Be brand brilliant

IT'S ALL ABOUT
INSTAGRAM
HASHTAGS

JULIE CHRISTIE-CLARK

BRANDING BY *Juls*

The purpose of using hashtags is not to get seen by a lot of people, it's about being seen by the right people

CONTENTS

Hello

Wow… it feels a wee bit surreal to write this, but welcome to my first book!

I'm Julie, and you might know me as the human (backed by my gorgeous pups, of course) behind Branding by Juls. I'm a Brand Designer and Strategist and I adore building brands that get to the essence of WHO and WHAT a business truly is.

I've worked in the world of branding and marketing for over 20 years and wouldn't change it for the world. I crave creativity, but love tapping into that with a strategic mind. For me, that's the sweet spot.

Helping and guiding people is what really fires me up. Maybe it's the Mum in me, but I believe there's nothing better than seeing people succeed. And that's what this book is all about.

Instagram can be an absolute game-changer for brands… but it's a tricky beast to navigate. Especially when it comes to hashtags, the options are endless and can stop people from even trying in the first place.

My mission is to break that right down for you and bring it back to basics. Because, curated correctly, hashtags could be your new BFF.

You can flick in and out of the different sections in the book to find the most relevant parts for you, and I've also included space at the back for you to make notes.

I'm so excited to hear what you think - feel free to pop me a message on Instagram **@brandingbyjuls**. Extra points for sharing any photos in your stories of you posing with the book that I can then share!

Until then - happy reading!

There's no avoiding it: Instagram hashtags are everywhere. But do you know how to use hashtags on Instagram to get the utmost value out of them for you and your brand?

We've all been there: you take and edit a photo, write a nice caption, use some hashtags, click share and hope for the best… only to hear crickets.

It's a beautiful photo. Your caption ticks all the boxes. And yet all you get is a handful of likes and maybe a throwaway comment.

Your heart sinks.

With the Instagram algorithm changing all the time, it's hard to get noticed and for your posts to even be seen. On average less than 10% of your own followers see your photos, let alone the rest of the Instagram world.

Sadly, you can't control the mysteries of the algorithm. Where it's heading is anyone's game.

What you can do is control and harness your hashtags.

And that's precisely what this book is all about! I'm here to guide you through the maze of hashtags so you can save hours and hours of research time. By the end, you will know how to pick the ones that fit like a glove and get your business seen by *all the right people*.

Because using relevant, brand specific hashtags on your posts and stories is one of the best ways to get discovered by new audiences on Instagram. If you aren't taking full advantage of these little gold mines, then you're seriously missing a trick.

Throughout this book you will uncover my library of meaningful, intentional and well thought out hashtags. These will help you save precious time so you can get back to focusing on your content, boosting your engagement and gaining that all important head start on growing your brand on Instagram.

BRANDING & VISIBILITY

It's simple: branding and visibility are the most effective uses of hashtags on Instagram.

While I hate to start things off with disappointment, let's lay things out on the table… it is impossible to list every single hashtag. There are MILLIONS out there covering every possible topic, business, hobby, lifestyle and favourite pet you can think of.

They've become a part of daily life. We use them when sharing photos, to find something specific, or simply out of boredom.

Which makes it a wee bit tricky to cover ALL of them… chances are there will always be some juicy ones you never even consider. But, if there's one thing the algorithm can't change, it's how and why hashtags are used.

That's why, now more than ever, it's crucial to pay them the attention they deserve. If you use them correctly, you can grow your brand, reach your dream clients and achieve your goal (whatever that might be!).

As a new business, you can use hashtags to expand your audience and increase brand awareness. Your aim should be to slot your branded posts into new people's (and potential customer's) Instagram feed. They'll see your posts, head over to your feed and hey presto, you could find yourself with a whole new set of followers. If you fail to use hashtags, your posts will only ever be seen by your current followers.

You can also create your own hashtag for your products or services, or even any events or competitions you are promoting. You can then encourage your followers and customers to use the hashtag whenever they purchase or use one of your products or services, or if they find themselves at your event or taking part in your competition.

This gives you the chance to dominate that hashtag with your brand. I use **#brandingbyjuls** and **#bebrandbrilliant** for my own branded hashtags. Continually using that hashtag in all your posts will help to increase your visibility, reach a larger audience and ensure people begin to associate your business with that hashtag.

The end result? A STRONGER more MEMORABLE brand that is unique and impactful.

USING BRAND RELEVANT HASHTAGS WILL HELP YOU TO:

✦ Improve the visibility of your posts

✦ Connect with like-minded business owners and individuals

✦ Gain followers

✦ Develop and grow your own community

✦ Build loyalty in your brand

But before we dive straight into 'all about the hashtags', you need to make sure you're confident in your own brand strategy.

Why does this matter? It will enable you to target your ideal audience on Instagram.

So, grab a cuppa, get comfortable and answer the brand questions on the next few pages. These will help you to focus on your 'why', what your offer is, your brand values and your brand vision.

You will also uncover your dream audience; the one your entire business is built to serve. Once you have these answers you can tailor your Instagram content and strengthen it with the very best, tailored hashtags.

You can then revel in:

✦ More comments

✦ More likes

✦ More impressions

✦ More sales, and…

✦ Even more sales!

Get brand
clarity

BRANDING ON INSTAGRAM

Instagram is the 'go-to' place if you want to learn more about a brand. Sure, they'll also check out your website if they're keen to really engage with you… but that tends to be after they've already decided whether you are someone they want to do business with.

So, what can you do to guide your ideal customer in that direction?

Your first step is your brand strategy. This is vital as it will give you the necessary insights into your customer needs, their wants, problems and pain points. Once you have a strong grasp on this, you can craft the most impactful messaging and content; the type that will turn them from curious leads to fully fledged, loyal consumers.

You'll find a series of questions over the next few pages: I want you to answer these as best as you can. This will enable you to truly understand what makes your brand unique and your business extraordinary. It will uncover your most important brand elements for your business, such as…

✦ Brand values

✦ Personality

✦ Target audience

…ensuring you can define and build a memorable, distinctive brand.

These answers will then form your reference guide, helping you deliver authentic, engaging content for your Instagram. You will also learn how to use hashtags in a strategic and consistent way, staying perfectly in line with your brand personality so that you can attract the people you dream of working with.

HISTORY

Why did you start your business journey?

Is there a unique story to your business? What is the meaning behind your business name?

COMPETENCY

What are your core strengths?

MISSION

Why does your business exist?

Why do you think people are drawn to your business, what makes you different?

REPUTATION

How would you like people to perceive your business when they see your brand?

How would you like people to feel after using your services or buying your products?

BUSINESS AIMS

What are your goals? Where do you see your business in 1 year? 5 years?

What is your niche?

Who are your main competitors (direct or indirect)? What to you think they do well? and not so well?

BRAND PERSONALITY

Make a mark on the line to distinguish how closely your brand aligns with the descriptions below.

TIMELESS ———————————————————— MODERN

RESERVED ———————————————————— EXCITING

ESTABLISHED ———————————————————— NEW

SOPHISTICATED ———————————————————— CASUAL

POLISHED ———————————————————— RUGGED

CORPORATE ———————————————————— PERSONABLE

SERIOUS ———————————————————— FUN

Identify where on the spectrum the majority of your marks are. This will help you define the high-level personality category for your brand. This exercise is a way for you to help identify what your brand personality really is.

BRAND BUZZWORDS

If your company were an individual person, how would you describe them?
Here are some suggestions, circle/highlight all that apply to you...

Adventurous	Approachable	Aspirational	Attentive
Authoritive	Balanced	Bold	Bubbly
Businesslike	Calm	Capable	Casual
Collaborative	Controlling	Corporate	Creative
Cutting edge	Daring	Dependable	Direct
Discrete	Distinctive	Distruptive	Dramatic
Energetic	Fearless	Focused	Formal
Friendly	Funny	High end	Honest
Imaginative	Impactful	Informal	Innovative
Inspirational	Inventive	Knowledgable	Laid back
Logical	Luxurious	Mindful	Motivated
Objective	Organised	Outgoing	Passionate
Patient	Practical	Proactive	Problem-solving
Professional	Progressive	Quirky	Relaxed
Resourceful	Romantic	Serious	Sincere
Sociable	Soft	Solid	Specialist
Stable	Strong	Thoughtful	Traditional
Trustworthy	Understated	Unique	Visionary

WHAT ARE YOUR CORE BRAND VALUES?

Your brand values are the guiding principles that help you connect with your target audience.

Ask yourself the following questions to help you define your brand values.

✦ How do you want your brand to be perceived?

✦ What's important about the way your run your business?

✦ How do you want your customers to feel when they work with you?

✦ What keeps you working on your business, what drives you day in day out?

✦ Why do you love what you do?

For example, mine are:

Distinctive - I aspire to deliver the best visual solutions, that are unique, luxurious and impactful

Bold - Be different, creating bespoke designs to make the perfect first impression and give my clients confidence in their business

Creative - I'm passionate about the power of strategic, intuitive brand design

CORE BRAND VALUES CONTINUED...

YOUR IDEAL CUSTOMER

Describe your ideal customer in as much detail as you can? (include male/female, occupation, where they live, their interests, what shops they like, car they drive, hobbies etc)

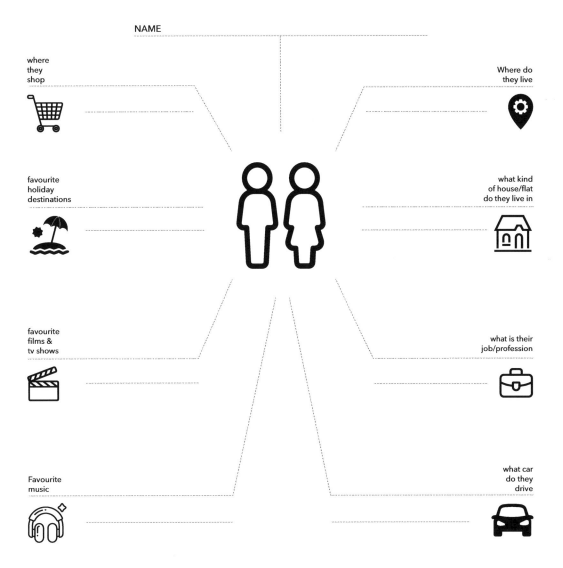

NAME

where they shop

Where do they live

favourite holiday destinations

what kind of house/flat do they live in

favourite films & tv shows

what is their job/profession

Favourite music

what car do they drive

ABOUT YOUR CUSTOMER
What are their biggest wants, needs and problems?

Name three specific ways you can help address their needs and solve their pain points?

Why do your customers trust you?

How do you make your customers feel?

IDEAL CUSTOMER PROFILE

So, now you've got the goods - it's time to pull it all together!

Look at everything you've written down and try to describe a typical day in the life of your ideal customer. I want you to think about:

What is their name?

How old are they?

Where do they live?

What are their favourite brands?

Who do they admire?

What do they do for a living?

How do they unwind?

What are their goals in life?

What are some of their wildest dreams?

This may feel slightly abstract - and take you out of your comfort zone! - but it's a brilliant way to have an actual human being in mind when you are crafting your communications. Whether it's on your website, your social media, your newsletter or any piece of marketing collateral, this profile will allow you to create direct dialogue between you and your ideal customer.

The end result? Content that is fully realised and 100% connects.

DESCRIBE YOUR IDEAL CUSTOMERS TYPICAL DAY...

CREATE YOUR VISION STATEMENT

What is your vision for your business...

For example: *I believe that everyone deserves a brand that feels 100% unequivocally them. I'm passionate about building brands that get to the essence of who and what a business truly is. Giving business owners the confidence to share their vision with a purpose driven, unique and captivating brand identity.*

CREATE YOUR MISSION STATEMENT

A *mission* is different from a *vision* – The vision statement focuses on tomorrow and what you want your business to become. The mission statement focuses on today and what the your business does.

For example: *My mission is to craft brand identities that truly reflect who you are. I seek to design strategic, creative and luxurious visual brand solutions that exceed market and customers' needs and expectations. Helping you feel proud of yourself, your business and the message you want to send out to the rest of the world.*

UNIQUE VALUE PROPOSITION

What is your UVP?

Also known as a unique selling proposition (USP), your UVP is a clear statement that describes the benefit of your offer, how you solve your customer's needs and what distinguishes you from the competition.

For example: *I am passionate about the power of strategic, intuitive brand design. Branding by Juls exists to inspire entrepreneurs who wish to make an impact in their business. To upscale and reach their dream audience with a luxurious, strategic and thoughtful visual brand identity.*

What exactly is a hashtag?

WHAT EXACTLY IS A HASHTAG?

Essentially, a hashtag is a label for content.

Hashtags hold the role of organising photos and videos on Instagram. They're pretty nifty; they're used to identify and file content on a specific topic, making it easier for your community and Instagram browsers to find you.

I picture it as a library or bookstore. Every book is slotted into a specific category, so whether you're after a bit of romance, a quick thrill or something meaty, you can find your book of choice quickly and with ease. Instagram hashtags do the same thing.

They're clickable, so anyone who clicks on an Instagram hashtag will be taken to a specific page that shows all the posts tagged with that hashtag. It can be a single word, an abbreviation, an invented combination of letters and numbers, or a phrase.

> Think of hashtags as little commmunities where your 'people' live.

Although they're fairly flexible, there are some points to keep in mind:

✦ If it is a phrase, there can be no spaces between words
  - all letters and numbers must run together without spaces

✦ You can't have punctuation or symbols in your hashtag
  (other than the # symbol at the beginning)

✦ Numbers are OK, but you must also have at least one letter with the numbers – hashtags cannot consist entirely of numbers.

So, now you know what a hashtag is and isn't… why would you want to use them in the first place?

WHY USE HASHTAGS?

You'll find hashtags on most social media platforms, but their greatest significance lies on Instagram. Anyone sharing content on a specific topic can add hashtags to their post. Then, if others are also searching for that topic, they will be drawn to your post. Ding ding, you'll immediately gain more eyes on your content.

Hashtags are how people find your posts when they are not already following you. They are therefore a fantastic way for you to connect with people who may not have come across your brand before.

People can also choose to follow hashtags which means your post could be channelled into their actual feed... even if they don't yet follow you.

Think of hashtags as little communities where your 'people' live. These 'people' are the ones who are MOST likely to comment, share or save your posts... they may then turn into loyal followers.

Why? If they're actively searching for that hashtag, it means they have similar interests, values and concerns. Consequently, they are FAR more likely to sit within your ideal target audience... aka the people who you want to get your content and posts seen by.

TRY TO GET INTO THE TOP POSTS

Have you noticed when you search a hashtag there are "top" and "recent" tabs?

These tabs are gold dust - it's the place you want to be.

But, as is life, those things that are *really* worth having are rarely easy to achieve.

You're battling against over 100 million new posts EVERY SINGLE DAY on Instagram; forcing your way into the top spot can't be done on a whim. It requires strategy and determination.

That's why you need to be deliberate and tactical with your choice of hashtags and use ones where you have the best chance to be in the top posts.

The best way to do that? Use smaller, targeted hashtags instead of the super popular, over-saturated ones.

With smaller, more niche hashtags you have more chance of being noticed and getting into the top posts and most importantly, staying there for longer.

TYPES OF INSTAGRAM HASHTAGS

PRODUCT OR SERVICE HASHTAGS: These are simple keywords to describe your product or service, like **#brandphotographer** or **#weddingcake**.

NICHE HASHTAGS: These are much more specific and relevant to your role within your industry, like **#copywriter** or **#crimewriter**.

COMMUNITY HASHTAGS: Instagram is a great way to find others in your own community and connect with them. Think **#floraldesignersofinstagram** or **#illustratorsofinstagram**.

CAMPAIGN HASHTAGS: Planning your next product launch, event or special offer? Create a campaign hashtag and encourage people to engage with it and use it, like Coca Cola's **#shareacoke** or ALS Association **#icebucketchallenge**.

BRANDED HASHTAGS: Branded hashtags are specific to your business, something simple could just be your business name, like **#brandingbyjuls**; this is a great way to make sure your posts relate back to your business and followers start to recognise your name. # weehappybox   # happy post everytime.

SPECIAL EVENTS/DAYS OR SEASONAL HASHTAGS: These can refer to holidays or seasons, like **#melodiesofspring** or they can be used for all those National Day holidays we all love and adore, like **#takeyourdogtoworkday** and **#internationalcatday**.

LOCATION HASHTAGS: It's always a good idea to include a hashtag or two that refers to your location, especially if you are a locally-based business, like **#glasgowcoffeeshop** or **#londonbeautician**.

ACRONYM HASHTAGS: Some well-known hashtags are **#TBT** for Throwback Thursday, there is also **#OOTD** for outfit of the day.

DAILY HASHTAGS: There are lots of hashtags for every day, from **#motivationmonday**, **#fridayintroductions** to **#lazysundaymorning**.

COMBINATION HASHTAGS: Adding words together is a great way to get your content seen by users across different demographics, like **#laptoplifestyle**, **#socialmediastrategist** and **#smallbizfamily**.

GENERIC HASHTAGS: These hashtags can relate to a specific industry, like **#coaching** or **#advertising** so that your posts are visible to users that have a general interest in your topic or market.

HIGH-DENSITY HASHTAGS: high-density just means the number of posts associated with a hashtag. If there are over 100 thousand and especially hashtags over 1 million, then this is high density.

LOW-DENSITY HASHTAGS: Low-density means hashtags that are more specific and reach a more targeted niche group. These groups usually have a more indepth interest in specific subjects or products and are likely to become engaged with your posts and have a higher chance of becoming a loyal follower.

HOW MANY HASHTAGS CAN I USE?

You can add up to 30 hashtags in your post, and 10 hashtags in a story. If you try to include more, your comment or caption won't post.

There is no right number of hashtags to use for your business. There are some experts who advise you to only use between 1 and 3 hashtags, some will say 11 is the optimum number... but I say, if Instagram allows you to use up to 30 hashtags then why not use them?

You may see some accounts with impressive followings but only a few hashtags in their posts. Don't let this deter you. If you are in the growing phase and aren't satisfied yet with the size of your following or the engagement that your posts are getting, then you should use all 30 hashtags. It may sound a lot, but every single hashtag you include into your posts can potentially grow your following and boost your business. And that's the ultimate aim, right?

TOP TIP
Be sure to make them relevant to your image, your brand and your audience.

Hashtags are the key to visibility. The algorithm is forever changing, and sometimes it will go against you (something that will NEVER be anything but infuriating), so the more hashtags you use, the better your chance of being noticed by someone who hasn't yet connected to your brand.

TOP INSTAGRAM HASHTAG POSTS

As of June, 2020, these are some of the top hashtags (otherwise known as high-density hashtags) on Instagram. But don't be fooled: most popular does not equal most effective.

These hashtags are so popular and over-used that your post will quickly become lost. My advice? Avoid them!

Some of the most overused Instagram hashtags include:

#love (1.82B)

#instagood (1.143B)

#fashion (807.1M)

#photooftheday (792.4M)

#beautiful (657.4M)

#art (643.6M)

#happy (576.9M)

#photography (575.9M)

#picoftheday (569.4M)

#cute (564.9M)

#follow (557.8M)

#travel (494.6M)

USE RELEVANT HASHTAGS

It's useful to group your hashtags together into set groups when you're building your hashtag strategy.

Start by asking yourself: what kind of content do you post about? You could be a food blogger… or maybe a personal trainer… perhaps you're a florist. Whatever category you fall into, make sure your tags are RELEVANT.

Remember; relevance applies to both that specific piece of content and your overall brand. People will immediately scroll on by if your post doesn't feel relevant to them. They can even report your post if you have used a hashtag which has nothing to do with your post image or content.

The key is that you aren't trying to trick people into liking you. As with all marketing, every move should be strategic and tailored around an audience that has a genuine interest in what you offer.

If you get this right, you'll not only grow your following much quicker - but you will have a more engaged and interested following who could turn into loyal fans: and that's what building a brand is all about.

AVOID USING THESE HASHTAGS

THE DESPERATE ONES

Avoid using hashtags that shamelessly look for likes and followers, like #follow4follow, #followme, #like4like etc. Using hashtags like these will attract bots, spammers and other users who are only interested in growing their own followers than ever showing a genuine interest in your business and engaging with you.

THE BLACKLISTED ONES

When inappropriate content becomes associated with a hashtag, Instagram might ban that hashtag. This doesn't mean you can't use it, it just means if you click on the hashtag, you will only see top posts. You won't see any recent posts. The only way to know if a hashtag is banned is to check it before you use it. This is good practice to put in place anyway as you don't want your posts to appear alongside others that don't quite fit with your brand values. Including a banned hashtag can cause a drop in engagement for your post.

THE SAME ONES

It may be tempting to use the same list of hashtags on every post, but don't. Instagram's community guidelines clearly state that 'posting repetitive comments or content' is not okay. If you use the same hashtags for every post, your content will be penalised by the algorithm. Instead, create at least 5-10 different hashtag sets that relate to the types of content you post for your business. There is space at the back of this book for you to write down your hashtag groups for easy reference. Once you have created your hashtag groups, save them in your notes section of your phone so you have them handy and just copy and paste every time you are creating a new post.

A few of the hashtag sets I have saved for easy access include: brand strategy, brand design, design blog, colour theory & moodboards, happy clients, my life, small biz & entrepreneur life and brand workshops.

MY HASHTAG FORMULA STRATEGY

Let me guess; you're feeling a bit confused about how to navigate the MANY different types of hashtags and have already given countless strategies your time and energy (to little avail)?

Well, why not give this one a try? It's a formula that has proven to be the most effective in growing my Instagram business account.

This strategic use of hashtags has significantly increased my chances of being featured among 'Top Posts' (these are the first nine posts you see when you tap 'Explore' and type in the hashtag you're searching).

TOP TIP

By including low-density hashtags that are niche and community-based means it is easier to rank and stay longer in Top Posts

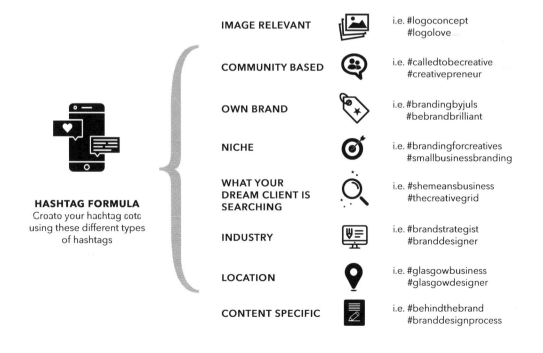

HASHTAG FORMULA
Create your hashtag sets using these different types of hashtags

IMAGE RELEVANT	i.e. #logoconcept #logolove
COMMUNITY BASED	i.e. #calledtobecreative #creativepreneur
OWN BRAND	i.e. #brandingbyjuls #bebrandbrilliant
NICHE	i.e. #brandingforcreatives #smallbusinessbranding
WHAT YOUR DREAM CLIENT IS SEARCHING	i.e. #shemeansbusiness #thecreativegrid
INDUSTRY	i.e. #brandstrategist #branddesigner
LOCATION	i.e. #glasgowbusiness #glasgowdesigner
CONTENT SPECIFIC	i.e. #behindthebrand #branddesignprocess

HASHTAG QUICK TIPS

THE BASICS

A hashtag needs to start with (#) plus a word or phrase. No spaces, no symbols.

FIRST THINGS FIRST

Make sure your profile is set to public otherwise your hashtags won't work: private accounts don't show up on hashtag feeds.

THINK LOCAL

Include location specific hashtags especially if you are a bricks and mortar business or are a local service.

MAGIC NUMBER

Use all 30 hashtags if you want too, there is no magic number to the best number of hashtags you should use, whether it is 2, 5 or 11!!! AND there are no penalties on engagement or reach by Instagram if you do use all 30, just remember quality over quantity is always best!

SWITCH IT UP

Don't use the same hashtags in every post, switch them up! Create between 5-10 different hashtag groups and keep them saved in your phone notes to copy and paste.

BEWARE OF SPAM

Avoid using hashtags that appear spammy eg. #likeforlike, #followme, #followforfollow, #love #quotes, #food, #mood etc.

Make sure your hashtags are relevant to your business, your post and the audience you want to attract.

KEEP IT RELEVANT

Avoid using the obvious, the overused and the over-saturated like #art, #design, #photography as they will have very little chance of being seen or reach the right audience. Niche down instead use #lifeofanartist, #designisinthedetails and #photographerslifeforme.

DON'T BE A GENERALIST

Hashtags can be used in your captions, comments, bios and Instagram Stories. You can place your hashtags into the first comment of your posts rather than the caption if you prefer, in order to separate the two.

USE THEM WISELY

Create your own brand hashtags. Do you have a big event, product launch or a new membership or service coming up? Make (and use) your own Instagram hashtags and encourage others to use them too. You could include a key hashtag associated with your brand in your bio so people will become familiar with it.

BE ON BRAND

Remember to include hashtags that target your potential clients and customers (your dream audience) rather than your peers and competitors.

KNOW YOUR AUDIENCE

TOP TEN
REASONS PEOPLE FOLLOW A BRAND ON INSTAGRAM

1 **INSPIRE CREATIVITY** - Your gallery feed is beautiful, memorable, engaging and full of consistently great branded content. Your grid stands out and leaves a lasting impression on followers and passers-by.

2 **BRAND INTRIGUE** - Let's face it, we humans are wee nosy parkers! We love to find out what's going on behind the scenes and we feel privileged when we get a sneaky peek. Instagram stories are the perfect place to let your followers glimpse a little into the faces behind your brand, your creative processes and previews to your new products or service launches.

3 **CUSTOMER SERVICE** - Social media is a brilliant platform to allow fans to sound off about a company's products and services… the good and the bad! These comments are guaranteed to be seen by the public and brands alike. However, how you respond to these comments can be a game changer, show sincerity, show a little humour too if you like but always respond to every comment and address any concerns quickly.

4 **BRAND CONNECTION** - Comment and like other accounts photos. People love to know who the personality is behind a brand; so reach out and make new, genuine connections; after all, this is what social is all about. Build new connections with other business owners , form future collaborations and find people who don't yet know about your brand.

5 **COMPETITION TIME** - You're running a challenge, giveaway or competition and they have to follow you to take part.

6 **BRAND LOYALTY** - People follow you because they like you... they really, really like you. People connect with brands that represent their own values, their ideal lifestyle and their personality. Whether your brand is fun, luxurious, cheeky, bold or corporate, be yourself and your content will attract and resonate with your target audience.

7 **BEAUTIFUL BRANDING** - You post great photographs and graphics. Instagram is a visual platform first and foremost, and so people will often be searching for compelling visual experiences that they can connect with emotionally.

8 **EXCLUSIVE DEALS** - People will follow you on social media so they will be the first to hear any exciting news released by your brand. It may be you offer them access to any special sales or promotions, reward them with a discount code or they are the first to hear an announcement on any new products or services you are launching. Customers love a deal and rewarding your faithful followers is a win, win to help you grow your brand loyalty.

9 **ENTERTAINING CONTENT OR INFORMATIVE CONTENT** - Instagram is a great platform for you to show off your brand personality and your area of expertise. By using those little squares to actually teach your followers, you are giving them a genuinely valuable experience and reason to follow you.

10 **FOLLOW FOR A FOLLOW** - They are following only in the hope you will follow back but you will find they either don't engage further with your account or swiftly unfollow a few days later. Annoying yes, but a common occurrence and just means they are not your ideal audience anyway.

TOP TEN
REASONS PEOPLE UNFOLLOW A BRAND ON INSTAGRAM

1 **YOU POST CONTENT THAT IS 'OFF-BRAND'** - If your business is all about delivering a slick, professional and reliable service, and then you suddenly start posting about a new crash diet you are on, or upload a drunken selfie taken at the weekend, it may clash with your brand values. As a result, those who follow you will likely hit the unfollow button.

2 **YOU POST INCONSISTENTLY OR TOO MANY PICTURES AT ONCE** - If you go for days or weeks without posting anything at all and then post 20 pictures in quick succession, you are going to annoy your followers; sorry to say it! Spread out your posts evenly whether once a day or 3 times a week for maximum impact and the best engagement.

3 **NOT FOCUSING ON QUALITY** - The quality of your images and graphics are poor or look unprofessional… unsurprisingly, this does nothing to showcase your brand and can give the impression that your products or services are low quality or unprofessional too.

4 **TOO SALESY** - You are posting too many sales or promotional posts; this is a surefire way of annoying a LARGE portion of your audience. Focus on creating more educational and entertaining content for your followers with a little sprinkle of promotional posts here and there.

5 **NOT BEING AUTHENTIC** - Your followers will quickly see through you if you are being less than honest or not a true reflection of your brand.

6 **YOU NEVER ENGAGE WITH YOUR FOLLOWERS** - Answer honesty, -do you always ensure you reply to every genuine comment you get on your posts or at least like them? Instagram is all about building connections and a sense of community around your brand. But relationships work both ways and you need to spend some time on your DMs and comments with your followers.

7 **SPAMBOTS** - If a spam or fake account has followed you, Instagram frequently deletes these types of accounts. If you suddenly lose a number of followers overnight, this might be why.

8 **FOLLOW/UNFOLLOW MERRY-GO-ROUND** - You will begin to spot the accounts who only follow you in the hope you will follow them back. This is why you often see your follower numbers rise and fall overnight.

9 **YOU POST SOMETHING A FOLLOWER DISAGREES WITH** - When you share a personal point of view you will find not all of your followers will always agree with you. Be careful of any damage to your brand reputation if you choose to post any content which may be controversial or offensive to some.

10 **YOU RECENTLY RAN A CHALLENGE, GIVEAWAY OR COMPETITION** - Some people will only have been interested in your brand for this one reason and unfollow soon after.

8 TYPES
OF INSTAGRAM POSTS

Do you always stick to posting just one image on your Instagram feed? Try to mix it up a little! Variety is the spice of life, and your audience craves content that stands out from the crowd. There are eight different types of content you can post on Instagram, crossing between image, animation, video and graphics. Each will have a different engagement rate with your audience… so why not experiment and see which one resonates the most?

TEXT BASED GRAPHIC

IMAGE

IMAGE CAROUSEL

INFOGRAPHIC

VIDEO

ANIMATED GIF

IGTV VIDEO
(MAX 10 MINS)

VISUALISED AUDIO

Content post & story planners

30 DAYS OF CONTENT & ACTIONS
FOR INSTAGRAM TO STRENGTHEN YOUR BRAND

When posting onto Instagram, before worrying about what hashtags to use - first you need to think about the content you are sharing and how to keep it relevant to your brand.

What can you post that will bring value to your followers, supporting your brand's message while also letting your followers know a little about you! the face behind your brand.

Instagram is the perfect opportunity to make a great first impression of your business and entice people to hit that 'follow' button. By creating a consistent brand story you can turn those casual visitors into devoted, engaged and loyal followers of your brand.

Here are 30 ideas to kickstart your Instagram content, allowing you to plan ahead, be consistent and build great engagement to help you reach your dream audience.

1. **HELLO**
   Let's get visible, when was the last time you appeared on your grid?

2. **ENGAGE**
   Go to your followers list and click on 10 of their profiles. Comment on their lastest post, try to do this daily. Then do the same for your follow list.

3. **AUDIENCE BUILDING**
   Follow 20 hashtags related to your target audience.

4.   BUILD CONNECTIONS
Engage in the new hashtags you are following, like and leave genuine comments, or even better, add value where you can.

5.   PROBLEM SOLVING
Share a critical problem that you solved for one of your clients.

6.   GOALS
Share a personal or business goal that you still hope to accomplish this year.

7.   SUPPORT OTHERS
Once a week give a shoutout to three small/local businesses you use, highlighting their amazing services/products.

8.   YOUR VALUES
What are your core brand values? What does your business stand for?

9.   INSPIRATIONAL
Who do you admire? Which brands do you love, why?

10.   POST A VIDEO
People connect with people, get your face seen and your voice heard!

11.   FEEDBACK
Ask your customers for feedback on your services. If they can leave you a testimonial/review on google even better!

12.   RESOURCES
What free resources do you have? Let your followers know what freebies you have available to download on your website.

13. **TUTORIAL**
    Show your audience how to do something that will help solve a problem they have.

14. **EPIC CONTENT**
    Take a topic in your area of expertise and write a detailed post or even better signpost to a more detailed blog and promote on Instagram.

15. **WHAT'S YOUR STORY?**
    Explain your brand story and your inspiration for starting your business.

16. **STAY MOTIVATED**
    How do you stay motivated? Any tips you can share that may help others stay focused?

17. **WEEKLY ROUND UP**
    Share some of your favourite posts from other brands you follow in your stories (remember to tag them so they can repost too).

18. **EXPERT TIP**
    Show off your expertise with a helpful tip!

19. **GO LIVE!**
    Be brave and go live.

20. **LESSON LEARNED**
    Share a business lesson learned (positive or negative).

21. **SHOUTOUT**
    Shoutout to a mentor or a hero.

22. BEHIND THE SCENES
Let your audience see a little peek behind the scenes of your biz.

23. YOUR WORKSPACE
Post a picture of your workspace.

24. MOTIVATING MONDAY
What are your goals for the week?

25. RECOMMENDATION
Recommend a fellow business to your audience.

26. BUSINESS BESTIES
Tag a friend or a business bestie who has supported you in your entrepreneurial journey!

27. SOULFUL SUNDAY
How do you relax? What do you get up to at the weekend?

28. INSPIRATIONAL QUOTE
Share an inspirational quote relevant to your brand personality.

29. VALUABLE RESOURCES
Share three resources/tools/apps you can't live without in your business.

30. THANKYOU
Thank your customers/followers for their support.

POST CONTENT
PLANNER

DAY	DATE / TIME	POST TYPE (image, video, igtv, gif, carousel, etc)	CONTENT TYPE (ie. educational, relatable, promotional etc)	CAPTION
MONDAY				
TUESDAY				
WEDNESDAY				
THURSDAY				
FRIDAY				
SATURDAY				
SUNDAY				

| CALL TO ACTION | TAGS/LINKS/COLLABS TO INCLUDE | IMPRESSIONS | LIKES | SAVES |
		REACH	COMMENTS	TOTAL ENGAGEMENT

POST CONTENT
PLANNER

DAY	DATE / TIME	POST TYPE (image, video, igtv, gif, carousel, etc)	CONTENT TYPE (ie. educational, relatable, promotional etc)	CAPTION
MONDAY				
TUESDAY				
WEDNESDAY				
THURSDAY				
FRIDAY				
SATURDAY				
SUNDAY				

CALL TO ACTION	TAGS/LINKS/COLLABS TO INCLUDE	IMPRESSIONS	LIKES	SAVES
		REACH	COMMENTS	TOTAL ENGAGEMENT

POST CONTENT
PLANNER

DAY	DATE / TIME	POST TYPE (image, video, igtv, gif, carousel, etc)	CONTENT TYPE (ie. educational, relatable, promotional etc)	CAPTION
MONDAY				
TUESDAY				
WEDNESDAY				
THURSDAY				
FRIDAY				
SATURDAY				
SUNDAY				

CALL TO ACTION	TAGS/LINKS/COLLABS TO INCLUDE	IMPRESSIONS	LIKES	SAVES
		REACH	COMMENTS	TOTAL ENGAGEMENT

POST CONTENT
PLANNER

DAY	DATE / TIME	POST TYPE (image, video, igtv, gif, carousel, etc)	CONTENT TYPE (ie. educational, relatable, promotional etc)	CAPTION
MONDAY				
TUESDAY				
WEDNESDAY				
THURSDAY				
FRIDAY				
SATURDAY				
SUNDAY				

CALL TO ACTION	TAGS/LINKS/COLLABS TO INCLUDE	IMPRESSIONS	LIKES	SAVES
		REACH	COMMENTS	TOTAL ENGAGEMENT

45 STORY PROMPTS
INSTAGRAM STORY IDEAS TO TRY OUT

Instagram Stories are a great way to interact with your followers and get your brand known to a wider audience. Including Instagram Stories should be part of your social content strategy. Here are 45 useful story prompts so you never run out of ideas. Remember, you can include up to 10 hashtags your story posts too.

1. A day in the life
2. An opinion about a current event
3. This weeks to-do list
4. Unboxing story
5. Use the poll or question sticker
6. Promote your product or service
7. Promote your freebie
8. 3 random facts about you
9. Share someone elses post that has inspired you
10. Share your progress on something
11. A one minute tutorial
12. Your morning routine
13. Shout out another business
14. Go live!
15. Share a before and after
16. Show behind the scenes or part of your business process
17. Current book you are reading
18. Promote a blog post
19. Share a goal you are working on

TOP TIP
Include a location tag to get more views to your story posts

20. How you 'reset' when you lose motivation
21. Something you are grateful for
22. Tools of your trade
23. A holiday that brings you joy or your happy place!
24. Your weekend plans
25. What you are currently watching on Netflix
26. A pump-up song you love
27. A new skill you are working on
28. A bad habit you are trying hard to break
29. Ask a question to learn about your followers
30. Biggest dissappointment in your biz
31. An important lesson you have learned in your biz
32. Funniest biz moment
33. One thing you wish you could re-do
34. Show your workspace
35. Have a wee rant about something!
36. Got a new launch coming up? post some teasers
37. Promote your latest post
38. Post a motivational quote
39. Share a testimonial from your customers/clients
40. Show off your success!
41. Completed a major project, got a huge sale? celebrate!
42. Promote your branded hashtag
43. Promote your other channels eg FB group, podcast, blog etc
44. Share some tips and tricks
45. Countdown to an event or a launch

STORY
POST SCHEDULE PLANNER

MONDAY	TUESDAY	WEDNESDAY	THURSDAY
...../...../.....	...../...../.....	...../...../.....	...../...../.....
☐ POSTED	☐ POSTED	☐ POSTED	☐ POSTED
☐ POSTED	☐ POSTED	☐ POSTED	☐ POSTED
☐ POSTED	☐ POSTED	☐ POSTED	☐ POSTED
☐ POSTED	☐ POSTED	☐ POSTED	☐ POSTED
☐ POSTED	☐ POSTED	☐ POSTED	☐ POSTED

FRIDAY	SATURDAY	SUNDAY
...../...../.....	...../...../.....	...../...../.....
☐ POSTED	☐ POSTED	☐ POSTED
☐ POSTED	☐ POSTED	☐ POSTED
☐ POSTED	☐ POSTED	☐ POSTED
☐ POSTED	☐ POSTED	☐ POSTED
☐ POSTED	☐ POSTED	☐ POSTED

NOTES

STORY
POST SCHEDULE PLANNER

MONDAY	TUESDAY	WEDNESDAY	THURSDAY
..../..../.....	..../..../.....	..../..../.....	..../..../.....
☐ POSTED	☐ POSTED	☐ POSTED	☐ POSTED
☐ POSTED	☐ POSTED	☐ POSTED	☐ POSTED
☐ POSTED	☐ POSTED	☐ POSTED	☐ POSTED
☐ POSTED	☐ POSTED	☐ POSTED	☐ POSTED
☐ POSTED	☐ POSTED	☐ POSTED	☐ POSTED

FRIDAY	SATURDAY	SUNDAY
..../..../....	..../..../....	..../..../....
☐ POSTED	☐ POSTED	☐ POSTED
☐ POSTED	☐ POSTED	☐ POSTED
☐ POSTED	☐ POSTED	☐ POSTED
☐ POSTED	☐ POSTED	☐ POSTED
☐ POSTED	☐ POSTED	☐ POSTED

NOTES

⬛ STORY
POST SCHEDULE PLANNER

MONDAY	TUESDAY	WEDNESDAY	THURSDAY
...../...../.....	...../...../.....	...../...../.....	...../...../.....
☐ POSTED	☐ POSTED	☐ POSTED	☐ POSTED
☐ POSTED	☐ POSTED	☐ POSTED	☐ POSTED
☐ POSTED	☐ POSTED	☐ POSTED	☐ POSTED
☐ POSTED	☐ POSTED	☐ POSTED	☐ POSTED
☐ POSTED	☐ POSTED	☐ POSTED	☐ POSTED

FRIDAY	SATURDAY	SUNDAY
...../...../.....	...../...../.....	...../...../.....
☐ POSTED	☐ POSTED	☐ POSTED
☐ POSTED	☐ POSTED	☐ POSTED
☐ POSTED	☐ POSTED	☐ POSTED
☐ POSTED	☐ POSTED	☐ POSTED
☐ POSTED	☐ POSTED	☐ POSTED

NOTES

45 CALL TO ACTION PROMPTS
FOR **YOUR INSTAGRAM POSTS**

A good instagram post should always end with a call to action. This allows you to build a relationship with your audience, add personality and inspire your followers to take action. Tell them to save, share, comment, tag or click through to your bio and hit the link. You should never presume your audience will know what you want them to do next, you have to give them an action to take.

1. Double tap if you…
2. Save this post…
3. Tell me how you…
4. Watch our stories for…
5. Send me a DM if you…
6. Grab this freebie…
7. Would you rather…
8. Giveaway time, enter to win…
9. Tag a friend who…
10. What do you do when…
11. I need your advice here…
12. Tell me about your…
13. Click the link in our bio for…
14. Head to our blog to find…
15. Come join us, find us on…
16. Tell me if you are the same as me…
17. Want to know all about…
18. Watch our story for…

19. Try it first…
20. Buy now…
21. DM now to reserve your space…
22. Follow me on…
23. Was this helpful? Share with…
24. What do you think about…
25. What is your favourite…
26. What would you do if…
27. Tag a… who needs to see this
28. Tag a… that inspires you
29. Tag someone who would look amazing in…
30. Do you know of any good…
31. Drop an emoji in the comments if…
32. Comment your favourite…
33. Discover how too…
34. Watch this video to learn more…
35. Share why you love…
36. Learn more about…
37. Sign up to our mailing list…
38. DM me for a chat…
39. Subscribe to my/our…
40. Get started…
41. Learn more...
42. Join us/me…
43. Let's start…
44. Claim your free…
45. Find out more…

POST & STORY
PLANNER NOTES

Engagement tracker

⬤ ENGAGEMENT
TRACKER

		WEEK 1	WEEK 2
	DATE		
AUDIENCE	TOTAL NUMBER OF FOLLOWERS		
	FOLLOWERS GROWTH (+/-)		
POSTS	TOTAL LIKES		
	TOTAL COMMENTS		
	TOTAL SHARES		
	TOTAL SAVES		
DISCOVERY	REACH		
	IMPRESSIONS		
INTERACTIONS	PROFILE VISITS		
	WEBSITE CLICKS		
	DIRECT MESSAGES		
	EMAILS		

WEEK 3	WEEK 4	WEEK 5	WEEK 6	WEEK 7

ENGAGEMENT
TRACKER

		WEEK 8	WEEK 9
DATE			
AUDIENCE	TOTAL NUMBER OF FOLLOWERS		
	FOLLOWERS GROWTH (+/-)		
POSTS	TOTAL LIKES		
	TOTAL COMMENTS		
	TOTAL SHARES		
	TOTAL SAVES		
DISCOVERY	REACH		
	IMPRESSIONS		
INTERACTIONS	PROFILE VISITS		
	WEBSITE CLICKS		
	DIRECT MESSAGES		
	EMAILS		

WEEK 10	WEEK 11	WEEK 12	WEEK 13	WEEK 14

ENGAGEMENT
TRACKER

		WEEK 15	WEEK 16
DATE			
AUDIENCE	TOTAL NUMBER OF FOLLOWERS		
	FOLLOWERS GROWTH (+/-)		
POSTS	TOTAL LIKES		
	TOTAL COMMENTS		
	TOTAL SHARES		
	TOTAL SAVES		
DISCOVERY	REACH		
	IMPRESSIONS		
INTERACTIONS	PROFILE VISITS		
	WEBSITE CLICKS		
	DIRECT MESSAGES		
	EMAILS		

WEEK 17	WEEK 18	WEEK 19	WEEK 20	WEEK 21

ENGAGEMENT
TRACKER NOTES

IT'S ALL ABOUT HASHTAGS

Creatives

CREATIVES

GENERAL

#abeautifulmess
#artiseverything
#blkcreatives
#calledtobecreative
#calledtocreate
#couragouscreative
#craftexposure
#createcultivate
#createlounge
#createinspirepositivity
#createthelifeyoulove
#createwithconfidence
#createyourhappy
#createyourreality
#createveryday
#creativeatheart
#creativebiz
#creativebusinessowner
#creativebusinessowners
#creativechics
#creativecontent
#creativecourage
#creativedirection
#creativeentrepreneur
#creativegoals
#creativehappenings
#creativehappylife
#creativeindustries
#creativeintroverts

#creativejournaling
#creativelife
#creativelifehappylife
#creativemedia
#creativeminds
#creativenomad
#creativepreneur
#creativesmallbiz
#creativesoul
#creativespace
#creativespirit
#creativeoninstagram
#creativethoughts
#creativitycoach
#creativityforlife
#creativityfound
#creativityiskey
#creativitymatters
#creatorslane
#darlingweekend
#dreamersanddoers
#everysquareastory
#handandhustle
#happycreativelife
#helpingcreativityflow
#herestothecreative
#herestothecreatives
#iamcreative
#independentmaker

#livecreatively
#livethelittlethings
#lovelysquares
#makersgonnamake
#makersmovement
#modernmaker
#mycreativebiz
#mycreativebusiness
#mycreativecommunity
#onmydesk
#peoplescreative
#postitforaesthetic
#risingtidesociety
#seekinspirecreate
#showyourmark
#supportthecreators
#thecreativegrid
#thenativecreative
#thiscreativelife
#timeforcreativesouls
#wanderleurspark
#wearethecreativecommunity
#wearethecreativeeconomy
#wearethemakers
#whereiwork
#whitespacefall
#whitespacespring
#whitespacesummer
#womencreatives

DESIGN

#advertisementdesign
#branddesign
#creativedesign
#currentdesignsituation
#dailydesign
#designadvice
#designalifeyoulove
#designandbuild
#designblog
#designconcept
#designdetails
#designdetailsmatter
#designerbags
#designerbrand
#designercakes
#designerclothes
#designerdresses
#designerfabrics
#designerfashion

#designerfurniture
#designerhome
#designerinspired
#designerjewellery
#designerlife
#designermaker
#designermonday
#designershoes
#designersofinstagram
#designessentials
#designeveryday
#designforeveryone
#designideas
#designinspiration
#designinspo
#designisinthedetails
#designlab
#designlove
#designlovefest

#designoftheday
#designsponge
#designstudio
#designthinking
#designtips
#designtrends
#designweek
#designyourlife
#designyourown
#gooddesignisforever
#instadesign
#interiordesign
#meetthedesigner
#simplycooldesign
#thedesigntalks
#thedesigntip
#untoldvisuals
#webdesign
#welovegreatdesign

GRAPHIC DESIGN

#brandidentitydesign
#brandlogo
#brandmark
#businessbranding
#businesscardsdesign
#businesslogo
#companylogo
#corporateidentity
#creativelogo
#customlogo
#customlogodesign
#dailyvector
#designinspiration
#digitalillustrations
#fontinspiration
#fontsmatter
#fontstyles
#fontswelove
#graphicdesignblog
#graphicdesignbook
#graphicdesigncentral
#graphicdesignclub
#graphicdesigncommunity
#graphicdesigndaily
#graphicdesignerlife
#graphicdesignerproblems
#graphicdesignersclub
#graphicdesignersgroup
#graphicdesignflow

#graphicdesigninspiration
#graphicdesignismypassion
#graphicdesignlife
#graphicdesignmemes
#graphicdesignportfolio
#graphicdesignservices
#graphicdesignstudent
#graphicdesignstudio
#graphicdesigntrends
#graphicgang
#graphicinspiration
#graphicoftheday
#graphicstudio
#greatlogo
#identitydesign
#illustrationdrawing
#kerning
#kerningfail
#learnlogodesign
#logo_showcase
#logoart
#logoawesome
#logobloom
#logobook
#logobrand
#logobranding
#logochallenge
#logocollection
#logoconcept

#logocreation
#logocreator
#logodaily
#logodesigner
#logodesigners
#logodesignersclub
#logodesigning
#logodesignlove
#logodesignprocess
#logoexcellent
#logofolio
#logogram
#logoguru
#logohero
#logoideas
#logoinspiration
#logoinspire
#logolearn
#logologo
#logolove
#logomania
#logomark
#logonew
#logopassion
#logoplace
#logoprocess
#logoroom
#logosai
#logoshop

#logosimple
#logotypeclub
#logotypes
#logowork
#logoworlddesigners
#minimalistdesign
#negativespace

#patternlove
#photoshop_art
#professionallogo
#surfacepatterndesign
#togetherweletter
#typedesign
#typefacedesign

#typehype
#typeposter
#typographyinspiration
#vector_art
#vectorlogo
#visualidentitydesign
#visualstorytelling

BRANDING

#behindthebrand
#brandambassador
#brandawareness
#brandbeautifully
#brandbrilliance
#brandbuilding
#brandcoach
#brandconsultant
#brandcreation
#brandculture
#brandcurated
#branddesigner
#branddevelopment
#brandedbags
#brandedcontent
#brandexpert
#brandguru
#brandidentity
#brandidentitydesign
#brandimage
#branding
#branding101

#brandingagency
#brandingcoach
#brandingdesign
#brandingforcreatives
#brandingidentity
#brandingimage
#brandinginspiration
#brandingmadeeasy
#brandingproject
#brandingstrategy
#brandingtip
#brandinspiration
#brandlaunch
#brandlogo
#brandmission
#brandofthebrave
#brandpersonality
#brandphotography
#brandrecognition
#brandrefresh
#brandstory
#brandstorytelling

#brandstrategist
#brandstrategy
#brandstyling
#brandstylist
#brandvalues
#brandvision
#brandyourbiz
#brandyourbusiness
#brandyourself
#buildyourbrand
#curateyourbrand
#lovelybrand
#modernbranding
#mybrilliantbrand
#personalbrand
#selfbranding
#smallbusinessbranding
#thebrandingcollective
#visualbranding
#welovebranding
#worldbranddesign
#youareyourbrand

WEBSITE DESIGN

#appdevelopment
#codeismylife
#codingdays
#codingfun
#codingislife
#codingproblems
#creatingwebsites
#creativecoding
#cssgrid
#dailyui
#dailyuichallenge
#dailywebdesign
#designweb
#devlife
#frontenddevelopment
#frontendfridays
#frontendwebdeveloper
#interfacedesign
#landingpagedesign
#landingpages
#mobileapplication
#mobiledesign
#newwebsitelaunch
#onlinepresence
#peoplewhocode
#responsivewebdesign
#searchenginemarketing
#searchengineoptimisation
#seoconsultant

#seotips
#squarespacecircle
#squarespacedesign
#squarespacedesigner
#uidesigner
#uidesignpatterns
#uitips
#userexperiencedesign
#userinterface
#uxdesigner
#uxdesignmastery
#uxuidesigner
#webdesignerlife
#webdesigns
#webdesignservices
#webdesignspecialist
#webdesignstudio
#webdesigntrends
#webdev
#webdeveloper
#webdevelopers
#webdevelopmentservices
#webhosting
#website_design
#websiteaudit
#websitebuilder
#websitecomingsoon
#websitecontent
#websitecopy

#websitedesignagency
#websitedesigning
#websitedevelopment
#websitehelp
#websiteinspiration
#websitemanagement
#websitemarketing
#websiteonline
#websiteoptimization
#websitephotography
#websiteranking
#websiteredesign
#websiteseo
#websiteservices
#websiteshop
#websitestudio
#websitetemplate
#websitetips
#websitetraffic
#woocommerce
#wordpresscommunity
#wordpressdevelopment
#wordpressexpert
#wordpressplugin
#wordpresstheme
#wordpresstips
#wordpresswebsite

ARTS & CRAFTS

#armknitthrow
#artforyourhome
#artismylife
#artistsofinstagram
#artsandcraft
#artsandcraftsforkids
#artsandcraftshome
#artsandcraftsmovement
#artsandcraftsstyle
#artsandcraftstime
#bewellandstitch
#buyhandmadegifts
#capturemycraft
#celebrate_handmade
#chooseartisan
#chunkyknit
#commercialart
#contemporaryembroidery
#craftbuzz
#craftingfun
#craftsfeed
#craftsposure
#crafttime
#createmakeshare
#creativecrewuk
#creatorslane
#crossstitchcrazy
#crossstitcher
#diyart

#embroiderylove
#favhandmade
#floralembroidery
#folksyshop
#girlsthatmakestuff
#handmadehour
#handmadeisbest
#handmadeisbestmade
#handmadeisbetter
#handmademovement
#handmadeparade
#handmaderevolution
#heattransfervinyl
#heytheremaker
#imadethat
#indiemaker
#inthestudio
#lovecrafts
#madetomatter
#makeallthethings
#makerlife
#makersgonnamake
#makersgottamake
#makersgunnamake
#makerslife
#makersmovement
#makersofig
#meetthemaker
#modernembroidery

#modernmaker
#modernmakers
#modernquilter
#ourmakerlife
#paperartist
#paperdecoration
#paperquillingartist
#prettycreativestyle
#quilledpaperart
#quillingartist
#quillingdesign
#quillinglove
#seekinspirecreate
#sharinghandmadejoy
#showyourwork
#slowstich
#supportlocalartist
#thehandmadeparade
#uniqueartwork
#useeveryscrap
#vinylcrafts
#waketomake
#wearethemakers
#weaversofinstagram
#wemakecollective
#whatimade
#workinprogress
#wovenart
#wovenwallhanging

ARTISTS & ILLUSTRATORS

#abstractdrawing
#acryliconcanvas
#animalartist
#asianartist
#artflowsessions
#artforinteriors
#artforthehome
#artforyoureveryday
#artinprogress
#artinspo
#artisticmoods
#artmotivation
#artscrowds
#artshare_ig
#artsupplies
#artsupplyaddict
#artworkdaily
#beboldbecreativebeyou
#blackartistspace
#blackartistsconnected
#botanicalart
#botanicalartlovers
#butterflyart
#carveouttimeforart
#contemporarydrawing
#contemporaryfineart
#dailydoseofpaper
#drawalot
#drawanyway

#drawdaily
#emergingartist
#expressiveart
#finelinedrawing
#floralillustration
#gouachepainting
#handmadepaint
#happyartistmovement
#happycreativelife
#iliketoartyhard
#illustratetheworld
#illustrationartistsofinstagram
#illustrationdaily
#illustrationgram
#illustrationnow
#illustrationoftheday
#iloveillustrators
#inkonpaper
#inspiredart
#inspiringwatercolours
#instaartwork
#inthestudio
#intuitiveart
#leafart
#lifeofanartist
#linedrawingart
#linedrawings
#livecolourfully
#livecreatively

#makearteveryday
#meettheartist
#newcontemporaryart
#paintanyway
#paintersofinstagram
#painteveryday
#paintingforsale
#paintingfromlife
#paintingfun
#paintingoncanvas
#paintingprocess
#paintingrocks
#paintingwithatwist
#paintpaintpaint
#passioncolourjoy
#penartwork
#pensketch
#peopleofprint
#prettyasapicture
#printmakersofinstagram
#realisticpainting
#studioscenes
#thenativecreature
#waltercolourflowers
#watercolorartist
#watercolourart
#watercolourlove
#watercoloursketch
#weloveillustration

COLOUR

#30daysofcolour
#beautifulcolour
#brandcolour
#brightcoloursmakemehappy
#color_of_day
#colorcrazy
#colorfulart
#colorharmony
#colorinspiration
#colorista
#colorjunkie
#colormix
#coloroftheday
#colorpalette
#colorswatches
#coloryourlife
#colour_guru
#colourblending
#colourchange
#colourcombinations
#colourcorrection
#colourcrazyme
#colourdrawing
#colourfulart
#colourful_shots
#colourfulclothes
#colourfulhome
#colourfullife
#colourfulpainting

#colouringforadults
#colourist
#colourit_up
#colourlove
#colourlover
#colourmehappy
#colourmelt
#colourmyhome
#colourofautumn
#colourofmylife
#colourofnature
#colourofphotography
#colourofspring
#colourofsummer
#colouroftheday
#colouroftheseason
#colouroftheyear
#colourofwinter
#colourpalettes
#colourpencils
#colourphotography
#colourplay
#colourpopme
#colourrun
#colourscheme
#colourspecialist
#coloursplash
#colourstory
#colourstreetphotography

#colourtheory
#colourtheory
#colourtherapy
#colourtrend
#colourway
#complimentarycolours
#contrastingcolors
#crashbangcolour
#dailydoseofcolour
#festivalofcolour
#fortheloveofcolour
#i havethisthingwithcolour
#ihaveathingforcolor
#ihavethisthingwithpink
#ilovecolour
#lifeisbetterincolor
#livecolorfully
#lovecolour
#metalliccolors
#myweekofcolour
#plantcolour
#popsofcolour
#softcolor
#splashofcolour
#thesecretlivesofcolour
#warmcolours
#welovecolour
#whywhiteworks
#yearofcolour

WRITERS

#authorslife

#autobiographical

#businessstorytelling

#contentcreationtips

#contentcreator

#contentmatters

#contentthatconnects

#contentthatconverts

#contentthatworks

#contentwriters

#contentwriting

#contentwriting

#copywriterlife

#copywritingtips

#crimefiction

#crimewriter

#digitalcontent

#entertainyouraudience

#everythingisacontentopportunity

#grammartips

#herwordisgold

#igwriter

#instagramwriters

#instawriter

#knowyouraudience

#marketingstories

#nonfiction

#nonfictionbooks

#poetrymonth

#rewriteyourstory

#richcontent

#screenwriter

#spilledink

#spilledwords

#storiesofmylife

#storiesmatter

#storiessell

#storiestotell

#storiesuntold

#storyteller

#storytelling

#storytellingforbusiness

#tellyourstory

#themodernstoryteller

#whatsyourstory

#wordhour

#wordsofwisdom

#wordswag

#wordswithkings

#wordswithqueens

#writergirl

#writergram

#writermemes

#writerproblems

#writers_around

#writers_den_

#writers_together

#writersblog

#writerscircle

#writerscommunity

#writerscommunityofinstagram

#writersconnection

#writerscorner

#writerslifeforme

#writersnetwork

#writersofig

#writersofinstagram

#writersoftheworld

#writerssociety

#writerssupportingwriters

#writersuniverse

#writewhatifeel

#writeyourblog

#writeyourstory

#writingtips

#yourstoryinstoveryet

#yourstorymatters

#yourstoryyourway

INTERIOR DESIGN

#apartmenttherapy
#beautifuldecorstyles
#bedroomstyling
#bohemiandecor
#bohoinspo
#brightspaceswelove
#charminghomes
#cleanaesthetic
#cornerofmyhome
#currenthomeview
#cushionaddiction
#dabblingwithdecor
#dailydecodetail
#dailydecordose
#decorcrushing
#delicousdarkdecor
#doingneutralright
#eclecticdecor
#farmhousechic
#farmhousefeels
#farmhousestyledecor
#farmhousevibesdecortour
#fixerupperstyle
#hallwayinspo
#heyhomehey
#homebeautiful
#homecanvas
#homedetails
#homeinspiration
#homeinspo

#homestylingideas
#howihome
#instainteriordesign
#interior123
#interior4all
#interiorandhomes
#interiordecoration
#interiordecorinspo
#interiordesignersofinsta
#interiordesigninspiration
#interiorstyling
#kitcheninspo
#laidbackluxe
#lifestylesoflivingspaces
#livingroomdecor
#livingroomgoals
#livingroominspo
#loungeroominspo
#loveinteriors
#luxeathome
#midcenturymodern
#mycolourfulinterior
#myeclecticmix
#mygorgousgaff
#myhomethismonth
#myhometoinspire
#myhometrend
#myhousebeautiful
#myhousethismonth
#mykindaplace

#myperiodhomestyle
#mystylishhome
#myvintageabode
#nestandthrive
#nesttoimpress
#neutraldecor
#nordicdesign
#nordicstyle
#openplanliving
#realinstahomes
#renovationlife
#rockmystylishhome
#rusticstyle
#sassyhomestyle
#scandihome
#scrollstoppinghome
#showusyourgaff
#simplystyleyourhome
#simplystyleyourspace
#smallspacesquad
#standoutstyling
#stopandstaredecor
#styledupinteriors
#styleitreal
#stylingmynest
#summerdecor
#thedelightofdecor
#therenovationcommunity
#walltowallstyle
#wherehomeisyourmasterpiece

FLORAL DESIGN

#(your city) + florist
#allthingsbotanical
#ayearinflowers
#beautifulblooms
#bloomandgrow
#bloomsoftheday
#blooooms
#botanicaldaydreams
#botanicalpickmeup
#bouquetoftheday
#daisiesaremyfavourite
#daysofmayflorals
#eventflowers
#fineartflorals
#floralarrangement
#floralartistry
#floraldecor
#floraldesignclasses
#floraldesignersofinstagram
#floraldesigns
#floraldesignschool
#floraldesignworkshop
#floralfix
#floralfun
#floralinspo
#florallife
#floralstories
#floralstyling
#floraltribute

#floristlife
#floristrymovement
#flowercrowns
#flowermagic
#flowerperfection
#flowersandotherstories
#flowersdaily
#flowersfordays
#flowersmakepeoplehappy
#flowersobsession
#flowersofig
#forflowerlovers
#fortheloveofflowers
#freshflowersmakemehappy
#giftofflowers
#givethegiftofflowers
#ihavethisthingwithflowers
#inspiredbyflowers
#inspiredbypetals
#inspirewithblooms
#jamjarposies
#justbefloral
#lavenderflowers
#lavenderlove
#lifeofaflorist
#localflorist + (your city)
#lushflowers
#luxuryblooms
#luxuryflowers

#mybunchofflowers
#peoniesaremyfavourite
#peonylove
#petalperfection
#petalsandprops
#plantsmakepeoplehappy
#prettyflowers
#propsandpetals
#realflorist
#realflowersoftheseason
#romanticflowers
#rosearemyfavourite
#seasonalbouqets
#seasonalfloweralliance
#sendflowers
#slowfloralstyle
#springblooms
#springblossoms
#stonefloralstyle
#studioflorist
#stylingtheseasons
#underthefloralspell
#uniqueflowers
#vaseofflowers
#weddingblooms
#weddingflorals
#whimsicalfloral
#wildflowermeadow
#wildflowerseason

TEXTILE / KNITWEAR DESIGN

#alwaysknitting
#fiberartfamily
#fibreart
#fibreartist
#getyourkniton
#handblockprint
#handknit
#handloomcotton
#handmadewardrobe
#handprintedfabric
#handprintedtextiles
#igknit
#iloveyarn
#knitaddict
#knitallthethings
#knitalong
#knitandbehappy
#knitdesign
#kniteveryday
#knitfastdiewarm
#knitinspiration
#knitinspo
#knitknitknit
#knitlife
#knitlove
#knitoholic
#knitpattern
#knitpatterndesign

#knitpicks
#knitsharelove
#knitshawl
#knitstyle
#knitters
#knittersgonnaknit
#knittersofig
#knittersofinstagram
#knittersoftheworld
#knitthat
#knitting_inspire
#knitting_is_love
#knittinginspiration
#knittingismysuperpower
#knittingismytherapy
#knittingismyyoga
#knittinglove
#knittingmakesmehappy
#knitweardesign
#knityourstyle
#lovetoknit
#modernweaving
#myfavouritethingsknitwear
#myfavouriteyarn
#nevernotknitting
#onemorerow
#onmyneedles
#ontheloom

#printandpattern
#slowtextiles
#sockknittersofinstagram
#sockknittingaddict
#sustainabletextiles
#textileartist
#textilearts
#textiledesigner
#textiledesignstudio
#textileinspiration
#textilelove
#textileoftheday
#textilepattern
#textileprints
#textiletuesday
#togetherweknit
#weareknitters
#wearyourknits
#weaverfever
#weaversofig
#weavingart
#woolart
#woventapestry
#woventextiles
#wovenwallart
#wovenwallhanging
#yarnandhook
#yarninspirations

CROCHET DESIGN

#crochetinspo
#colourfulcrochet
#crochet_relax
#crochetaddict
#crochetallday
#crochetanddo
#crochetanimal
#crochetblogger
#crochetclothes
#crochetcommunity
#crochetcreator
#crochetcrew
#crochetdesigns
#crochetdoll
#crochetersofinstagram
#crochetersoftheworld

#crocheteveryday
#crochetforbaby
#crochetgeek
#crochetgirlgang
#crochethandmade
#crochethappiness
#crochetingthroughlife
#crochetinspiration
#crochetismyyoga
#crochetlifestyle
#crochetlove
#crochetmakesmehappy
#crochetmood
#crochetpatterns
#crochetsocietystar
#crochettherapy

#crochettoy
#crochetwip
#crochyay
#fashioncrochet
#hooknookers
#ilovecrochet
#instacrochet
#instacrocheting
#moderncrochet
#mosaiccrochetblanket
#stylishcrochet
#whatsonmyhook
#whatsonyourhook
#yarnaddict
#yarninspiration
#yarntherapy

POTTERY MAKER

#britishpottery
#ceramicart
#ceramicarts
#ceramicsaretrending
#ceramicslove
#claytherapy
#contemporaryceramics
#freshfromthekiln
#functionalpottery
#handbuiltceramics
#handbuiltpottery
#handmademugs
#handmadeplates
#handmadepottery
#hobbypotter
#ihavethisthingwithceramics
#instapottery
#kilncasting
#kilnfired
#kilnfolk

#kilnformed
#loveclay
#lovemakingpottery
#modernceramics
#polymerclaylove
#potsinaction
#potteryart
#potteryartist
#potterycafe
#potteryclass
#potterycollector
#potterydesign
#potteryfixation
#potteryforall
#potteryglaze
#potterygram
#potteryheart
#potterykiln
#potterylessons
#potterylife

#potterylove
#potterymug
#potterypainting
#potteryplace
#potteryplate
#potteryprocess
#potteryschool
#potterystudio
#potteryvase
#potteryvideo
#potterywheel
#potterywheelthrowing
#potteryworks
#potteryworkshop
#stonewareceramics
#stonewarepottery
#studioceramics
#studiopotter
#studiopottery
#wheelthrown

BAKERS + CAKE DESIGN

#amazingcupcakes
#anniversarycake
#awesomecakes
#babyshowercake
#bakeandshare
#bakersspotlight
#bakeyourworldhappy
#bakingfromscratch
#bakingtherapy
#bakingwithlove
#beautifulcakes
#bespokecakes
#bespokeweddingcakes
#birthdaycakeideas
#birthdaycakesformen
#buttercreamcakes
#buttercreamflower
#buttercreamlove
#cakeart
#cakeartistry
#cakebirthday
#cakedecor
#cakedecoration
#cakedecorationideas
#cakedecorator
#cakeideas
#cakeinspiration
#cakeinstagram
#cakelove
#cakeloversdelight

#cakemasters
#cakepop
#cakepopstagram
#cakepopart
#cakepopcake
#cakepopcuties
#cakepopmaker
#cakepoplove
#cakepopsicles
#cakepopstand
#cakery
#cakes + (your city)
#cakesdaily
#cakeselfie
#cakesforalloccasions
#cakeshop
#cakesiclesofinstagram
#cakesinstyle
#cakesmash
#cakesquad
#cakestagram
#cakesthatwow
#cakestyle
#caketoppers
#caketrends
#cakevendorsconnect
#cakevideo
#castlecake
#charactercakes
#chocolatecupcake

#chocolatedripcake
#contemporaryweddingcakes
#cookiecake
#cupcakeart
#cupcakebouquet
#cupcakeday
#cupcakedecorating
#cupcakelove
#cupcakeproject
#cupcakequeen
#cupcakevideo
#cutecake
#decoratingcakes
#dessertoftheday
#deliciouscakes
#dripcakesofinstagram
#elegantcakes
#elegantweddingcakes
#fancycake
#flowercakes
#flowercupcakes
#freshlybaked
#glazedcake
#howtocakeit
#ilovebaking
#instabake
#instacupcakes
#kiddiescakes
#lovebakingcakes
#luxurycakes

#luxuryweddingcake
#madefromscratch
#marblecake
#minicakes
#moderncakes
#perfectpiping
#pipingflowers
#pipingskills
#pipingtechniques
#premiumcake
#prettycakes
#princesscake

#professionalbaker
#rainbowcake
#rosecupcakes
#seminakedcake
#simplecake
#strawberrycake
#sugarflowerart
#sugarflowerartist
#sugarflowers
#sugarflowersbouquet
#sugarroses
#superherocake

#sweetcravings
#theweddingcakediaries
#undiscoveredbaker
#uniquecakes
#vanillasponge
#victoriaspongecake
#weddingcakedesign
#weddingcakegoals
#weddingcakeideas
#weddingcakeinspiration
#weddingcakeinspo
#weddingdesserttable

CANDLE MAKER

#allnaturalsoycandles
#artisancandles
#beeswaxcandles
#bookcandle
#bookishcandles
#candlecommunity
#candlemaker
#candleobsessed
#candlesaddict
#candlescented
#candlescents
#candleseason
#candlesfordays
#candlesglamour
#candleshop

#candlesofinstagram
#candlesticks
#candlestore
#candlestudio
#candlesuk
#citruscandle
#cleanburningcandles
#crystalcandles
#essentialoilcandles
#handmadecandles
#handpouredcandles
#herbalcandles
#homefragrance
#homemadecandles
#ilovecandles

#imperialcandles
#luxurycandles
#luxuryhomefragrance
#makingcandles
#naturalcandles
#pillarcandles
#scentedcandles
#soyblend
#soycandlesforsale
#soywaxcandles
#springcandles
#vegancandles
#waxmeltaddiction
#waxmeltuk
#woodenwickcandle

JEWELLERY DESIGN

#accessorydesigner
#animaljewelry
#anklebracelet
#artisanmade
#artjewellery
#asianjewellery
#beadedbracelet
#beautifuljewelry
#beautifuljewellery
#beautifuljewels
#bespokejewellery
#bespokering
#birdjewelry
#bohoearrings
#botanicaljewelry
#braceletformen
#bracelethandmade
#braceletlove
#braceletoftheday
#braceletsfemme
#braceletsforwomen
#braceletstacks
#braceletswag
#braceletystyle
#bridaljewellerydesigns
#bridaljewelleryset
#bridaljewels
#broach
#broochlover
#charmbracelets

#clayearrings
#contemporaryjewellery
#contemporaryjewels
#copperearrings
#custompendant
#customring
#daintybracelet
#daintyearrings
#daintyjewellery
#daintynecklace
#daintyrings
#dangleearrings
#destinationjewellery
#diamondbracelet
#diamondjewellery
#diamondpendant
#diamondsareforever
#earringdesign
#earringsaddict
#earringset
#earringsfashion
#earringshandmade
#earringslove
#earringsofinstagram
#earringsogood
#earringstyle
#ethicaljewellery
#ethnicearrings
#finejewellery
#forestjewelry

#friendshipbracelet
#gemstonebracelet
#gemstoneearrings
#glasspendant
#goldbracelet
#goldearrings
#goldjewellery
#goldjewellerydesign
#goldpentant
#goldrings
#goldsmith
#handcraftedearrings
#handmadebrooch
#handmadejewelleryuk
#handmadependant
#healingjewelry
#heartpendants
#heirloomjewelry
#hoopearrings
#indianjewels
#instajewellery
#instasmithy
#jewellersatwork
#jewellersofinstagram
#jewellery_blog
#jewelleryartist
#jewellerybox
#jewellerybrand
#jewellerycollection
#jewellerycollectors

#jewelleryfashion
#jewellerygram
#jewelleryinspiration
#jewellerylove
#jewellerymaker
#jewellerymakers
#jewellerymonthly
#jewelleryobsessed
#jewelleryoftheday
#jewelleryonline
#jewelleryphotography
#jewellerysale
#jewelleryset
#jewelleryshop
#jewellerystyle
#jewellerytrends
#jewelleryworkshop
#jewelryaddict
#jewelrylover
#jewelrymaking
#jewlerydesign
#jewlerydesigner
#jewleryoftheday
#junkjewellery
#ladysmiths
#lifeofajeweller
#metalsmithing

#metalsmithsociety
#namependant
#natureinspiredjewelry
#naturejewelry
#oneofakindjewellery
#onmybench
#pakistanijewellery
#partyjewellery
#pearljewellery
#pendantearrings
#pendantlove
#pendantnecklace
#pendantoftheday
#pendantsets
#polymerclayearrings
#quirkyjewellery
#receptionjewellery
#resinearrings
#rhinestonejewelry
#ringbling
#ringgoals
#ringoftheday
#ringring
#ringsofinstagram
#ringsoftheday
#ringstack
#rosegoldengagementring

#rosegoldeverything
#rosegoldjewellery
#rosegoldjewelry
#rosegoldring
#shelljewellery
#silverearrings
#silvergold
#silverpendant
#statementbracelet
#statementearrings
#statementjewellery
#statementjewels
#sterlingsilverearrings
#stoneearrings
#traditionalearrings
#traditionaljewellery
#turquoiseearrings
#uniquejewellery
#vintagejewellery
#vintagejewelleryforsale
#vintagejewelrylover
#vintagejewels
#weddingjewellery
#weddingjewellerytrends
#weddingjewelleryset
#weddingjewels
#wrapbracelet

WEDDING PLANNER

#aisledecor
#aislegoals
#aislestyle
#bohoinspiredwedding
#bohowedding
#bohoweddinginspo
#bouquetgoals
#bridaltable
#bridetobe_(year)
#ceremonydecor
#classicwedding
#countryhousewedding
#dayofcoordinator
#destinationelopement
#destinationweddingplanner
#diywedding
#easyweddings
#elegantweddings
#eventcoordinator
#eventinspiration
#eventspecialist
#futuremrandmrs
#imgettingmarried
#indiewedding
#instawedding
#itsallinthedetails

#justsaidyes
#lgbtmarriage
#lgbtproposal
#loveisntcancelled
#luxewed
#luxurywedding
#luxuryweddingplanner
#luxuryweddings
#marryingmybestfriend
#nauticalwedding
#outdoorweddings
#planningawedding
#proposalideas
#realweddings
#rockmywedding
#romanticwedding
#rusticwedding
#smallweddings
#tablescapes
#theknotrealweddings
#tietheknot
#tohaveandtohold
#ukwedding
#weareengaged
#weddingcenterpieces
#weddingcentrepiece

#weddingceremonydecor
#weddingchairdecor
#weddingchairs
#weddingcoordination
#weddingcoordinator
#weddingdaycoordinator
#weddingfloral
#weddinggoals
#weddinginspo
#weddinglocations
#weddingparty
#weddingplannerlife
#weddingplanners
#weddingplanningbegins
#weddingplanningtime
#weddingplanningtips
#weddingreceptionideas
#weddingstyling
#weddingtablesetting
#weddingtrends + (year)
#weddingvenuehunting
#weddingvenues
#weregettingmarried
#youyourwedding

EVENT STYLING

#anniversarydecor

#babyshowerideas

#balletparty

#balloonarch

#balloonarrangement

#balloonbackdrop

#balloonbouquet

#balloondecor

#balloondecorator

#balloondelivery

#balloondesigner

#balloongarland

#balloongift

#ballooninspiration

#ballooninstallation

#balloonqueens

#balloonsculpture

#balloonstylists

#balloonsurprise

#balloonwall

#beautifulevents

#bespokeballoons

#bespokeevents

#bespokeevents + (your city)

#birthdayballoons

#brandparty

#bridalshowerdecor

#bubbleballoons

#corporateeventstyling

#customballoons

#customparty

#decoinspo

#decorationlovers

#decorinspiration

#engagementdecor

#engagementdecoration

#eventinspo

#eventmanagement

#events + (your city)

#eventsandadventures

#eventsdecor

#eventsdesign

#eventservices

#eventsindustry

#eventslife

#eventsmanagement

#eventsorganising

#eventspace

#eventsphotographer

#eventsplannedwithlove

#eventsspecialist

#eventstyling

#eventsupplier

#eventtips

#eventtrends

#flowerwall

#gardenparties

#henpartydecor

#hottrends

#letterballoons

#luxuryballoons

#luxuryevent

#luxuryeventdesign

#luxuryeventdesigner

#luxuryeventplanner

#luxuryeventplanners

#luxuryevents

#luxuryparties

#organicballonarch

#organicballoongarland

#organicballoons

#partyplanning

#partystyling

#romanticdecoration

#rosegoldballoons

#staircasedecor

#sustainabledecor

#tabletopdecor

#weddingballoons

#wowfactor

STATIONERY DESIGN

#bespokeinvitations
#bespokestationery
#bulletjournaljunkies
#couturenotebook
#custominvites
#customstationery
#customweddingstationery
#cutestationery
#dailydoseofpaper
#decklededge
#digitalnotebook
#eventstationery
#foilinvitations
#fortheloveofpaper
#handmadebook
#handmadegreetingcards
#handmadenotebook
#letterpressprinting
#luxuryinvitations
#luxurystationery
#moderntableplan
#notebook_profile
#notebookaddict
#notebookart
#notebookcovers
#notebookcustom
#notebookdesign

#notebookdoodles
#notebookers
#notebookhardcover
#notebooking
#notebooklove
#notebooktherapy
#onthedaystationery
#paperaddict
#papernerd
#personalisedseatingchart
#planneraddict
#pocketnotebook
#prettypaper
#semicustominvitation
#stationeryaddict
#stationeryaddicted
#stationeryaddicts
#stationeryblogger
#stationerydesign
#stationerydesigner
#stationeryflatlay
#stationeryfreak
#stationerygeek
#stationerygoals
#stationerygoodies
#stationeryhaul
#stationeryhoarder

#stationeryholic
#stationeryjunkie
#stationerylove
#stationerylovers
#stationerynerd
#stationeryset
#stationeryshop
#stationeryshopping
#stationeryshow
#stationerystore
#stationerytrends
#studyinspiration
#studymotivation
#styledstationery
#tableplaninspo
#thenotebook
#travellersnotebook
#weddinginviteinspo
#weddingpaper
#weddingstationer
#weddingstationery
#weddingstationeryboss
#weddingstationerydesign
#weddingstationeryideas
#weddingstationeryinspiration
#weddingstationeryuk
#welovepaper

CALLIGRAPHY

#beginnerscalligraphyworkshop
#bespokecalligrapher
#brushscript
#calligrapher
#calligraphersofinstagram
#calligrapheruk
#calligraphy_art
#calligraphy_daily
#calligraphyart
#calligraphyartist
#calligraphybasics
#calligraphychallenge
#calligraphycommunity
#calligraphydesign
#calligraphyforbeginners
#calligraphygang
#calligraphyinspired
#calligraphylesson
#calligraphylettering
#calligraphyletters
#calligraphylove
#calligraphylover
#calligraphymasters
#calligraphynewbie

#calligraphypractice
#calligraphyquote
#calligraphysign
#calligraphytattoo
#calligraphytools
#calligraphytutorial
#calligraphyvideo
#calligraphyworkshop
#calligraphywriting
#copperplatecalligraphy
#customcalligraphy
#dailycalligraphy
#envelopeaddressing
#envelopeart
#envelopecalligraphy
#eventcalligrapher
#fauxcalligraphy
#handemadefont
#handlettered
#handletteringart
#handletteringpractice
#handtypography
#learncalligraphy
#letsdolettering

#letterart
#lettering
#letteringart
#letteringartist
#letteringcommunity
#letteringdaily
#letteringgoodvibes
#letteringlove
#letteringwithpositivity
#letterlove
#lovecalligraphy
#moderncalligraphy
#moderncalligraphyuk
#modernlettering
#nomoreboringenvelopes
#onsitecalligrapher
#pointedpen
#pointedpencalligraphy
#showusyourlettering
#thedailycalligraphy
#togetherweletter
#typegang
#weddingcalligrapher
#weddingcalligraphy

LANDSCAPE DESIGN

#gardentransformation
#backyarddesign
#backyardgoals
#beautifulhomes
#cornerofmygarden
#cottagegardenstyle
#cutflowergarden
#dreamhomes
#eatwhatyougrow
#enjoyyourgarden
#exteriordesign
#flowersmakemehappy
#frontgardendesign
#functionalgarden
#gardenart
#gardenbed
#gardendecor
#gardendesigner
#gardendesigninspiration
#gardendesignlove
#gardendesigns
#gardendesignuk
#gardenersofig
#gardenersworld
#gardenflowers
#gardengoals
#gardengreatorsmall
#gardeningisfun
#gardeningisgoodforthesoul
#gardeningismytherapy

#gardeningtips
#gardeninguk
#gardenkitchen
#gardenlandscaping
#gardenlove
#gardenlovers
#gardenmaintenance
#gardenpatio
#gardenpots
#gardenprojects
#gardensculpture
#gardensofinsta
#gardenspace
#gardentransformation
#getyourhandsdirty
#greenfingers
#growyourownveg
#happygardener
#happygardeninglife
#hardlandscaping
#homeandgarden
#howdoesyourgardengrow
#indiansandstone
#kerbappeal
#landscapearchitecture
#landscapedesign
#landscapedesigner
#landscapedesignideas
#landscapegoals
#landscapingideas

#loveyourgarden
#makingmydreamgarden
#moderngarden
#mygardenthismonth
#myrealgarden
#naturalstone
#newbuildgarden
#newgarden
#outdoordesign
#outdoorentertaining
#outdoorentertainingarea
#outdoorkitchen
#outdoorliving
#outdoorlivingspace
#palletfurniture
#patiodecor
#plantingtips
#potagergarden
#raisedbedgardening
#raisedbeds
#raisedgardenbeds
#smallgardenideas
#smallgardens
#steppingstones
#stonewalkway
#summergardens
#urbangardendesign
#vegetablegardening
#veggiepatch
#womeninagriculture

PHOGRAPHY

#allbeauty_addiction
#awesome_photographers
#best_silhouette
#bestofvsco
#brandingimage
#brideandgroomphotos
#britphotographerscollective
#calledtobecreative
#chasinglight
#citypictures
#cityshot
#clickmagazine
#clickpro
#collectivelycreate
#dearphotographer
#depthoffield
#documentaryphotgraphy
#documentingdays
#documentyourdays
#fearlessphotographers
#featurepalette
#gatheredstyle
#goldenratio
#harmonyoflight
#HDRspotters
#hellostoryteller
#honestlydocumented
#icatching
#ig_great_pics

#ig_myshot
#iglobal_photographers
#infilmwetrust
#inspiremyinstagram
#justgoshoot
#leadinglines
#let_there_be_delight
#lettherebedelight
#lifeofaphotographer
#lightinspired
#lightphotography
#liveforthestory
#longexposure
#lookslikefilm
#lovelysquare
#makeportraits
#monochrome
#moodyfilm
#mybestcityshots
#myfeatureshoot
#photodaily
#photog
#photografy
#photografyday
#photografylovers
#photographerproblems
#photographerscollective
#photographerslife
#photographerslifeforme

#photographerslifestyle
#photographerslove
#photographersoninstagram
#photographyaddict
#photographyeveryday
#photographyislife
#photographyismylife
#photographysouls
#photosinbetween
#portrait_perfection
#portraitcollective
#portraitmood
#portraitoftheday
#portraits_ig
#portraits_universe
#portraitstyles
#postthepeople
#propstyling
#propstylist
#pursuepretty
#pursuitofportraits
#reflectiongram
#rsa_portraits
#seekthelight
#sepiaphotography
#shotwithcanon
#shotoniphone
#shotwithlove
#shotwithmoment

#shotzdelight
#simpleandstill
#still_life_gallery
#stillswithstories
#stockimages
#stockphotographer
#stockphotos
#styledshoot
#styledstockphotography

#styledstockphotos
#thehonestlens
#thelifestylecollaborative
#thesincereststoryteller
#thevisualscollective
#thiswildlingsoul
#thoughthelens
#townphotography
#untoldvisuals

#urbanshot
#viewpoint
#vintagephotographs
#vintagephotography
#vintagephotos
#visualsoflife
#wanderlust
#worldbest_shot
#yourockphotographers

WEDDING PHOTOGRAPHY

#(your city) + weddingphotographer
#brideandgroomphotos
#couplesphotographer
#destinationphotographer
#destinationweddingphotographer
#documentaryweddingphotography
#editorialweddingphotographer
#elopementphotographer
#engagementphotography
#fineartfilmweddingphotographer
#fineartweddingphotography
#intimateweddingphotographer
#loghtandairyphotography
#luxuryweddingphotographer
#quirkyweddingphotography

#relaxedweddingphotography
#thisisreportage
#travelweddingphotography
#vintageweddingphotography
#weddingdaydetails
#weddingfilm
#weddingphotography
#weddingphotography + (your city)
#weddingphotoinspiration
#weddingphotos
#weddingphotoshoot
#weddingportrait
#weddingportraits
#weddingstories
#wedphotoinspiration

FLATLAY PHOTOGRAPHY

#bookflatlays
#coffeeflatlay
#creative_flatlays
#creativeflatlays
#creativelysquared
#flatlay_foodie
#flatlay_gallery
#flatlay_moment
#flatlayaddict
#flatlayart
#flatlaybeauty
#flatlaybreakfast
#flatlaycoffee
#flatlaycosmetics
#flatlaydaily

#flatlayfan
#flatlayfashion
#flatlayfeatures
#flatlayflowers
#flatlayfood
#flatlayfoodies
#flatlayforever
#flatlayfriday
#flatlaygoals
#flatlayinspiration
#flatlaylove
#flatlaymakeup
#flatlaynation
#flatlayoftheday
#flatlayout

#flatlayphoto
#flatlayphotography
#flatlaysquad
#flatlaystudio
#flatlaystyle
#flatlaystyling
#flatlaytea
#flatlaythebest
#flatlaythenation
#flatlaytoday
#floralflatlay
#mywhitetable
#stillswithstories
#teaflatlay
#theflatlaysquad

PRODUCT PHOTOGRAPHY

#advertisingphotography
#commercialphotographer
#contentphotography
#filmlights
#filmlighting
#foodbackground
#foodphotography
#foodstylingbackgrounds
#photofood

#photographyandstyling
#photographystudio
#productphoto
#productphotographer
#productphotography
#productphotos
#productphotoshoot
#productshot
#productshotoftheday

#productshoot
#productstyling
#productstylist
#propphotographer
#propstylist
#stilllifephoto
#stilllifephotographer
#studiolight
#studiophoto

FAMILY PHOTOGRAPHY

#babyphotoshoot

#bestnewbornphotographer

#birthphotographer

#birthphotography

#clickingmoms

#familiesonfilm

#familyphotographer + (your city)

#familyphotographers

#familyphotographynow

#familyphotographysession

#familyphotoideas

#familyphotosession

#familyphotoshoot

#familyphotoshoots

#familypicture

#familyportraits

#familysession

#inhomesession

#lifeandlensblog

#lifestylefamilyphotography

#lifestylenewbornphotography

#lifestylephotographers

#livejoyphotography

#lookslikefilmkids

#maternityphotographer

#maternityphotoshoot

#minisessions

#mommyandmephotoshoot

#motherhoodphotography

#motherhoodsessions

#newbornphoto

#newbornphotographer

#newbornphotography

#newbornphotographyprops

#newbornphotos

#newbornpictures

#newbornposing

#photographyprops

#pocket_sweetness

#rose_colored_childhood

#thebabyyears

#thefamilynarrative

#theheartcaptured

#thelifestylecollective

#themindfulapproach

#thesincerestoryteller

#thesweetlifeunscripted

#toddlerphotography

BRAND PHOTOGRAPHY

#(your city) + headshotphotographer
#brandimages
#brandingphotographer
#brandingphotography
#brandphoto
#brandphotographer
#brandphotography
#brandphotos
#brandphotoshoot
#brandsession
#brandstory
#buildyourpersonalbrand
#businessbranding
#businessbrandingphotography
#businessheadshots
#businessphotographer
#businessphotography
#businessportraits
#commercialphotographer
#corporateheadshots
#headshotcrew
#headshotphotographer
#headshotphotography
#headshots
#headshotsession
#headshotsonly

#headshotstudio
#personalbranding
#personalbrandingphotography
#personalbrandphotographer
#personalbrandphotography
#photographyfriends
#photographyfun
#portraitinspiration
#portraitphoto
#portraitphotographer
#portraits_ig
#portraits_today
#portraits_vision
#portraitshots
#portraitsquad
#portraitvisuals
#professionalheadshots
#seniorphotographer
#showtherealyou
#smallbusinessbranding
#smallbusinessphotographer
#smallbusinessphotography
#socialcurator
#topheadshotphotographer
#visualstoryteller
#youareyourbrand

VIDEOGRAPHER

#adobepremiere
#aerialvideography
#animationdesign
#behindthescene
#behindthescenegram
#behindthescenes
#brandedvideo
#cameragear
#cameragirl
#cameraoperator
#camerasetup
#camerawoman
#cinemacamera
#cinematographylife
#colograde
#commercialvideography
#creativelight
#creativevideo
#directorslife
#dronevideography
#eventvideography
#fashionvideography
#femalefilmmaker
#femalefilmmakers
#femalevideography
#filmakersworld
#filmcommunity
#filmediting
#filmfeed

#filmingtips
#filmlife
#filmlook
#filmmakerslife
#filmmakersworld
#filmmaking
#filmproduction
#followfocus
#framegrab
#freelancevideographer
#greenscreenstudio
#lifeonset
#motiondesigner
#motiongraphicscollective
#motionmate
#motionprocess
#movieclips
#onlyfilmmakers
#phonevideography
#premierepro
#preweddingvideography
#productionlife
#professionalvideo
#realestatevideography
#setlife
#socialmediavideo
#travelvideography
#videobranding
#videobusiness

#videochat
#videocontentmarketing
#videodiary
#videoediting
#videoeditors
#videoforbusiness
#videogamephotography
#videograph
#videographerlife
#videographers
#videographylife
#videographywedding
#videomaking
#videomarketing
#videoshoot
#videoskills
#videostaredits
#videostory
#videostudio
#videotutorial
#visualcreators
#visualdesign
#visualsoflife
#weddingvideographer
#weddingvideography
#womaninfilm
#woodencamera
#xclusiveproduction
#youngfilmmakers

IT'S ALL ABOUT HASHTAGS

Lifestyle

LIFESTYLE

GENERAL

#abmlifeisbeautiful
#abmlifeissweet
#alifeofintention
#alittlebeautyeveryday
#aquietstyle
#artofslowliving
#asecondofwhimsey
#astilllifestyle
#beautifulmatters
#beautifulmemories
#beautifulmess
#beautifulmind
#beautifulmoment
#beautifulmoments
#beautyinsimplicity
#beautyundermynose
#beautyyouseek
#buildalifeyoulove
#calm_collected
#confidencebooster
#consciousculture
#consciouslife
#consciouslifestyle
#createthelifeyoulove
#createthelifeyourway
#creativehappylife
#curatedlife
#dailymotivation
#darlingdaily

#darlingmoments
#daysofsimpleandslow
#daysofsmallthings
#distractionsandinspirations
#documentyourdays
#dowhatyoulove
#dreaminginpictures
#elegantexcellence
#finditliveit
#findyourepic
#findyourhappy
#findyourshine
#findyourtribe
#folkcreative
#friendsinmyfeed
#getoutofyourownway
#getunstuck
#goalswithsoul
#gratefulheart
#happinesswithin
#heartandhustle
#holdyourmoments
#howiseeit
#howyouglow
#inspirationdaily
#inspirationoftheday
#inspiredwomen
#inspiringwomen
#its5oclocksomewhere

#kindredmemories
#lifeonpurpose
#livecolourfully
#liveinspired
#livelaughlearn
#livethelittlethings
#liveunscripted
#liveyourpurpose
#lovelysquares
#makewaves
#margaritatime
#momentslikethese
#momentsofmine
#morningslikethese
#mybeautifulmess
#mydarlingminimal
#myeverydaymagic
#myquietbeauty
#myquietplace
#mystoryoflight
#mytinymoments
#myunicornlife
#naturally_imperfect
#ohtheheart
#onthedesk
#onthetable
#postitforaesthetic
#posttheordinary
#productivityhacks

#pursueyourpassion
#reclaimthehappy
#rockyourbliss
#sayyestosuccess
#searchwandercollect
#seekinspirecreate
#seekmoments
#seeksimplicity
#seekthesimplicity
#shareyourstory

#shedesignedalifesheloved
#shepreneur
#showupasyou
#simpleliving
#simplethingsmadebeautiful
#slowdownwithstills
#slowlivingforlife
#tellyourstory
#thatauthenticfeeling
#theeverygirl

#thehappynow
#theslowdowncollective
#thoughtleader
#todayslovely
#welivetoexplore
#whywhiteworks
#worklifebalanced
#yourstory
#yourstorymatters
#yourstoryyourway

QUOTES

#aestheticquotes
#bestsayings
#cutesayings
#entrepreneurquotes
#funnysayings
#inspirationalquote
#inspirationalsayings
#inspirationalwords
#inspiringquotes
#instathought
#lifequotestoliveby
#lifesayings
#lovesayings
#motivationalsayings
#motivationalwords
#motivationquote
#positivesayings
#postivewords
#quotes4you
#quotesaboutlove

#quotesandsayings
#quotesbyme
#quotesdaily
#quotesforher
#quotesforhim
#quotesforsuccess
#quotesforyou
#quotesilove
#quoteslife
#quoteslove
#quotesofinsta
#quotesoflife
#quotestoliveby
#quotestolivebyforever
#quotestoremember
#quotesworld
#sayingsandquotes
#sayingsoftheday
#sayingstoliveby
#successfulquotes

#successquote
#thoughtsinwords
#truesayings
#wisesayings
#wordsandsayings
#wordsarepowerful
#wordsforthought
#wordsgram
#wordsofadvice
#wordsofaffirmation
#wordsofencouragement
#wordsofig
#wordsofinspiration
#wordsoftheday
#wordsoftruth
#wordstoinspire
#wordstoliveby
#wordstoponder
#wordswithmeaning
#wordswordswords

INSPIRATIONAL/MOTIVATIONAL

#abundancemindset
#accountabilitybuddy
#accountabilitygroup
#actiontaker
#aspiretoinspire
#attitudeofgratitude
#beamazingeveryday
#beboldbeyou
#bestfeelingever
#beunstoppable
#boldbraveyou
#breathedeep
#cherishedmoments
#dailymotivation
#dontbringmedown
#dontquityourdaydream
#dowhatsetsyoursoulonfire
#dreambigdreams
#dreambigorgohome
#dreambigworkhard
#earnyourhappy
#elevatecultivate
#endlesspossibilities
#findingyourfearless
#findyourvision
#findyourwhy
#fuelthesoul
#futureisbright
#futureisbrighter
#goalgetters
#goalslayer
#goalswithsoul

#goforgreatness
#goodinspirations
#goodvibrations
#gottastayfocused
#gratefulday
#gratitudeattitude
#growyourself
#hustle101
#icaniwillwatchme
#instagood
#intentionallife
#itsgoodtotalk
#itsthelittlethings
#joyfuljourney
#keepgoingforward
#keepupthegoodwork
#keepyourchinup
#livelifeonyourterms
#liveyourpassion
#lookingforhappiness
#lovingkindness
#makeithappen
#meaningfulconversations
#mindsetforgreatness
#mindsetgrowth
#mindsetiskey
#mindsetmastery
#mindsetmattersmost
#mindsetmotivation
#mindsetshift
#mindsetwork
#motivationalquote

#myownbosslife
#notlookingback
#opportunityawaits
#ownyoureveryday
#paystobebrave
#progressnotperfection
#pursueyourpassion
#setgoalsnotlimits
#shareyourwins
#shedidit
#sheisnotlost
#shootforthestars
#showingupforme
#showingupformyself
#showupasyou
#showupeveryday
#slaytheday
#stateofpositivity
#stayinspired
#striveforsuccess
#successmindset
#taketheleap
#theambitionplan
#thisisyourtime
#thoughtsbecomethings
#timetoshine
#workforwhatyouwant
#youcandoanything
#yourjourneystartshere
#yourowntime
#yourstoryyourway
#youweremadeformore

FAMILY

#alwaysthereforme

#babiesandpuppies

#babieslove

#babiesofinsta

#babiesoninstagram

#babybliss

#babyrolls

#candidchildhoodunplugged

#cheekygirl

#childrenseemagic

#cutebabyclub

#familyandfriends

#familycomesfirst

#familyfirst

#familyfriendly

#familygathering

#familygoals

#familyguy

#familyhistory

#familyholiday

#familyhome

#familyiseverything

#familyisforever

#familyislife

#familylove

#familymoment

#familymoments

#familymovienight

#familyouting

#familyowned

#familyphoto

#familyreunion

#familyselfie

#familytimefun

#familytimeisthebesttime

#familytimeisqualitytime

#familytimepriceless

#familytimes

#familytimesarethebest

#familytradition

#familyvacation

#familyvalues

#familyweekend

#fullhandsfullheart

#gummygrin

#habitandhome

#heartisfull

#holdthemoments

#ilovemyfam

#ilovemyfamilysomuch

#inbeautyandchaos

#instababylove

#letthembelittle

#lookatthatface

#lookatthatsmile

#lovemyfam

#lovemykids

#lovethemtobits

#luckytohaveyou

#meandmygirl

#missingmyfamilysomuch

#mycuprunnethover

#myhearts

#mytinytribe

#our_everyday_moments

#ourtinymoments

#parentingmemes

#parentingwin

#purelyauthenticchildhood

#sleepinglikeababy

#somuchdrool

#takemyheart

#takemyheartdear

#takemyhearteverywhere

#tenfingers

#tentoes

#theartofchildhood

#thefamilynarrative

#thesincereststoryteller

#toocuteforwords

#toocutetohandle

#toocutenottopost

#toocutenottoshare

#toocutethough

#toocutetuesday

#wouldnthaveitanyotherway

#writeyouonmyheart

MUM LIFE

#(your city) + mum
#busymum
#firsttimemum
#firsttimemummy
#ecomum
#honestmum
#mumandbaby
#mumanddaughter
#mumblog
#mumboss
#mumdiaries
#mumgoals
#mumlife

#mumlifeisthebestlife
#mumlifeuk
#mummakeup
#mummies
#mummyandbaby
#mummyandme
#mummybloggeruk
#mummytobe
#mumpreneurs
#mumshustlehard
#mumslife
#mumsofinstagramuk
#mumssupportingmums

#mumstagram
#mumstyle
#mumswithcameras
#mummydiaries
#newmum
#raisingtinyhumans
#stylishmum
#tiredmummy
#tiredmumsclub
#ukmumblogger
#ukmums
#ukmumsquad
#veganmum

MOM LIFE

#momgoals
#cuddleswithmommy
#honestmom
#honestmomconfessions
#honestmommin
#imacoolmom
#lifeasmom
#modernmom
#mombloggers
#momanddad
#momcommunity
#momcrushmonday
#momfashion
#momitforward

#momlifebalance
#momlifebelike
#momlifeishard
#momlifekeepingitreal
#momlifestyle
#momlifeunfiltered
#momllifestyle
#momlofebestlife
#momlove
#mommydiaries
#mommygoals
#mommylifestyle
#mommylove
#mommymoments

#momproblems
#momsofboys
#momssupportingmoms
#momstrong
#momstruggles
#momsunite
#momswithmuscle
#momtrepreneur
#momtruth
#momtruths
#momunity
#momwin
#overwhelmedmom
#unitedmomsnetwork

MOTHERHOOD

#blessedmother
#bloggingmama
#dailymamamoment
#documentingmotherhood
#heaventhroughmylens
#honestlymothering
#instamamasupport
#intentionalmotherhood
#lifeasmama
#lifewithlittles
#magicofmotherhood
#mamahoodinsquares
#mammahoodsisterhood
#messy_motherhood
#momentsinmotherhood
#motherhood_squares
#motherhoodandme
#motherhoodbliss
#motherhoodcommunity
#motherhoodcorner

#motherhoodinspired
#motherhoodinsquares
#motherhoodinstyle
#motherhoodintheraw
#motherhoodisdarling
#motherhoodishard
#motherhoodismagic
#motherhoodlens
#motherhoodlife
#motherhoodrocks
#motherhoodsisterhood
#motherhoodstruggles
#motherhoodthroughig
#motherhoodthroughinsta
#motherhoodtruths
#motherhooduncut
#motherhoodunfiltered
#motherhoodunhinged
#motherhoodunite
#motherhoodunited

#motherhoodunplugged
#motheringittogether
#mothermusing
#mummalife
#mummalove
#mummasboy
#mummasgirl
#mymamahood
#mynameismama
#newmama
#notonlymama
#ohheymamas
#ohmamamoment
#realmotherhood
#simplymamahood
#storytellingmama
#theartofbeingamother
#thismamaloves
#thismammaloves
#welcometoparenthood

SELF CARE

#acceptyourself
#alifeofintention
#bekindtoyourself
#chillaxing
#choosehappiness
#dayoffwellspent
#embracechange
#enjoyinglifetothefullest
#enjoythemoments
#feelingrelaxed
#getawayfromitall
#goodforthesoul
#healingmyself
#healthyboundries
#intention
#intentionallife
#intentionalliving
#intentions
#intentionsetting
#itsoktosayno
#keepgoing
#livewithintention
#lookingafterme
#lookingaftermyself
#mentalwellbeing
#mindsetcoach

#mindsetiseverything
#mindsetshift
#mindshift
#mywayofrelaxing
#nourishyourself
#personaldevelopment
#personalgrowth
#positive_energy
#positive_vibes
#positiveaffirmations
#positiveenergy
#positivelife
#positivemind
#positivemindset
#positivevibesonly
#positivityiskey
#positivityonly
#positivityquotes
#powerofintention
#powerofpositivity
#rechargeyoursoul
#relaxandunwind
#relaxifyoucan
#relaxmode
#relaxmoment
#restandrejuvenate

#restandrelaxation
#selfbelief
#selfcare101
#selfcareday
#selfcareeveryday
#selfcarefirst
#selfcaregoals
#selfcareishealthcare
#selfcareisnotselfish
#selfcarematters
#selfcaresaturday
#selfcaresunday
#selfcaretips
#successdiaries
#successfulwomen
#successmindset
#successquotes
#successstory
#successtip
#successtips
#switchingoff
#timeoutforme
#timetochill
#wellbeing
#wellnesswednesday
#youareworthy

SPIRITUALITY

#abundance

#affirmations

#angelguidance

#awakethesoul

#awakenedsoul

#dailyguidance

#divineenergy

#divinefeminineenergy

#divinefemininerising

#divineguidance

#divinelyguided

#divinetiming

#divinewisdom

#findyourcalling

#findyourhappiness

#findyourpath

#findyourpeace

#findyoursoul

#goddessenergy

#healingenergy

#heartcentered

#highervibes

#highvibe

#highvibetribe

#highvibration

#highvibrations

#innerknowing

#intuitivecoach

#intuitiveguidance

#lawofattraction

#lawofattractionquotes

#lawofvibration

#lifepurpose

#liveyourtruth

#loveandlight

#manifest

#manifestation

#manifestationbabe

#manifestdaily

#manifestdestiny

#manifesting

#manifestingdreams

#manifestingmagic

#manifestyourdreams

#mindbodyspirit

#mindsetofgreatness

#moneymindset

#openyourheart

#powerofnow

#powerofthemind

#powerofthought

#presentmoment

#raiseyourfrequency

#raiseyourvibration

#soulfulliving

#souljourney

#soulpreneur

#soulpurpose

#soultribe

#spiritjunkie

#spiritualawakening

#spiritualbadass

#spiritualbosslady

#spiritualentrepreneur

#spiritualgangster

#spiritualgrowth

#spiritualgrowthjourney

#spiritualjourney

#spiritualquotes

#spiritualwisdom

#synchronicity

#theuniversehasyourback

#trustyourintuition

#trustyourpath

#trusttheuniverse

#vibratehigher

#womanwithavision

#yourvibeattractsyourtribe

BOOKS AND READING

#alwaysreading
#amreading
#averybookishpost
#beautifulbooks
#betterwithbooks
#bookaddict
#bookaddiction
#bookaesthetic
#bookaholic
#bookalicious
#bookandcoffee
#bookbabe
#bookbag
#bookblog
#bookblogger
#bookbuzz
#bookclub
#bookdragon
#bookgeek
#bookgram
#bookgrammer
#bookie
#bookishfeature
#bookishlove
#bookishphotography
#booklovers
#bookloversunite
#booknerd
#booknerdigans
#booknerds

#booknook
#booknookstagram
#bookofthemonthclub
#bookphotography
#bookpile
#booksandcoffee
#booksandshares
#booksaremagic
#booksaremylife
#booksbooksandmorebooks
#booksbooksbooks
#bookshelf
#booksmakemehappy
#booksofinstagram
#booksonbooks
#bookspines
#bookstagram
#bookstagramcommunity
#bookstagramfeature
#bookstagrammer
#bookster
#bookworld
#bookworm
#businessbooks
#coffeeandcurrentreading
#cozyreading
#currentlyreading
#epicreads
#fortheloveofbooks
#fortheloveofreading

#goodreads
#greatread
#greatreads
#iread
#ireadbooks
#ireadeverywhere
#librarylove
#nevernotreading
#rainbowshelves
#readallthebooks
#readerlife
#readersofinstagram
#readingaddict
#readingbooks
#readingfestival
#readinghabits
#readingiscool
#readingisfun
#readingislife
#readingissexy
#readinglist
#readinglove
#readingnook
#readingtime
#readingtips
#somanybookssolittletime
#spreadthebooklove
#whatareyoureading
#whattoread
#whattoreadnext

TRAVEL

#adventure_time
#adventureseeker
#aroundtheglobe
#awesomeearthpix
#beautifulexplorers
#dametraveller
#dream_spots
#dreamingtravels
#exploreourearth
#exploringtheglobe
#femmetravel
#getlostclub
#girlaroundtheworld
#girlaroundworld
#girlsaroundtheworld
#girlsborntotravel
#girlsthatwander
#globalcapture
#globe_travel_
#globelletravels
#globewanderer
#hello_worldpics
#huffpostravel
#iamatraveller
#ilovetraveling
#inspiredtravels
#instatravelling
#ladiesgoneglobal
#letsflyawayto

#lifewelltravelled
#livetotell
#mydomaintravels
#ontheroadagain
#passionpassport
#passportexpress
#passportlife
#passportready
#postcardsfromtheworld
#searchwandercollect
#sheisnotlost
#sidewalkerdaily
#suitcasetravels
#takemethere
#the_daily_traveller
#thedreamytravels
#theprettycities
#thetraveler
#thetravellersway
#thetravellerwomen
#thetraveltribe
#thetravelwomen
#travel_captures
#travel_drops
#traveladdicted
#travelanddestinations
#travelandlife
#travelawesome
#travelbrilliantly

#traveldreamseekers
#travelforever
#travelforlife
#travelgirlsgo
#travelguide
#travelholic
#traveljournal
#travelingthroughtheworld
#travellovers
#travellust
#travelnow
#travelpassion
#traveltheglobe
#travelvibes
#vacationforever
#vacationland
#vacationlife
#vacationmode
#vacationready
#vacationstyle
#vactiongoals
#wanderluster
#wanderlusting
#wdestinations
#weekendwanderlust
#wonderlusting
#worldtravelescapes
#worldtraveladdict
#worldwonder

FITNESS

#aerialmovement
#agilitytraining
#armbalance
#athomestretches
#betterforit
#bodyweightworkout
#caloriedeficit
#circuitworkout
#everydamndayfitness
#findyourbalance
#findyourfit
#findyourpeak
#findyourstrength
#findyourstrong
#fitnessaddict
#fitnessblog
#fitnessblogger
#fitnesscoach
#fitnessfamily
#fitnessfirst
#fitnessforlife
#fitnessfreak
#fitnessfriday
#fitnessgirlsmotivation
#fitnessgoal
#fitnesshumour
#fitnessinspiration
#fitnessinspo
#fitnessinstructor
#fitnessjourney

#fitnessjunkie
#fitnessmeals
#fitnessmotivation
#fitnessmum
#fitnesstips
#fitnesstrainer
#fitnessvideo
#flexibilityandstrength
#flexibilityclass
#flexibilitycoach
#flexibilitydrills
#flexibilityexercises
#flexibilitygoals
#flexibilityinprogress
#flexibilityiskey
#flexibilityjourney
#flexibilityprogress
#flexibilitytips
#flexibilitytrainer
#flexibilitytraining
#flexibilitywork
#functionalfitness
#functionalrangeconditioning
#getbendywithgravity
#gluteworkout
#hipmobility
#kettlebelltraining
#kettlebellworkout
#liftheavyeatclean
#liftheavyliftoften

#liftheavyorgohome
#liftheavyrepeat
#liftheavyrunfast
#lowerbodystrength
#mobilitydrills
#mobilityexercises
#mobilitytraining
#movebetterfeelbetter
#movementcoach
#movementpractice
#muscleandstrength
#powertraining
#rangeofmotion
#resistancebands
#resistancetraining
#shouldermobility
#shoulderworkout
#sportsphysio
#sportsphysiotherapy
#strengthbuilding
#strengthconditioning
#strengthening
#strengthstartshere
#strengthtrainingforwomen
#stretchingroutine
#strongandflexible
#trainsmart
#trainwithpurpose
#upperbodyworkout
#workoutoftheday

YOGA

#(your city) + yoga
#acroflow
#acroyoga
#acroyogachallenge
#acroyogafun
#acrvinyasa
#advancedyoga
#aerialyoga
#ashtangalove
#blackyogalife
#dailyyoga
#dailyyogachallenge
#dailyyogapose
#dailyyogapractice
#doyouyoga
#flexibilityyoga
#forwardfold
#gentleyoga
#goddesspose
#halflotuspose
#headstandpractice
#howtoyoga
#idoyogasoidontkillpeople
#inflexibleyogis
#kickassyoga
#moreyogaplease
#onlineyogaclasses
#standinghalflotus
#sunsalutation
#warrior2

#yoga + (your city)
#yogaanywhere
#yogaathome
#yogabalance
#yogabeginner
#yogabody
#yogabusiness
#yogachallenge
#yogachallenges
#yogaclassonline
#yogacommunity
#yogacouple
#yogaeverybeautifulday
#yogaeveryblessedday
#yogaeverydamndaily
#yogaeverydamndaygoals
#yogaeverymoment
#yogaeverymorning
#yogaeverysingleday
#yogaeverytime
#yogaeverywhereigo
#yogafail
#yogafitnessinspo
#yogaforanxiety
#yogaforbalance
#yogaforbackpain
#yogaforbeginners
#yogaforeveryone
#yogaforfitness
#yogaforflexibility

#yogaforrecovery
#yogaforsleep
#yogaforthesoul
#yogafriends
#yogahigh
#yogahumor
#yogainspiration
#yogaismagic
#yogajournal
#yogalifelessons
#yogalifehappylife
#yogalifeme
#yogalifestyle
#yogalifetips
#yogalifeyogainspiration
#yogamakesmehappy
#yogamotivation
#yogamum
#yogaoutdoors
#yogaoutside
#yogaposes
#yogapractice
#yogaprogress
#yogaquotes
#yogaretreat
#yogateacher
#yogateachers
#yogateachertraining
#yogatherapy
#yogaworld

HEALTH

#eatinghealthier
#fitterhappierhealthier
#goodhealth
#goodhealthalways
#goodhealthandwellbeing
#goodhealthisgoal
#goodhealthiswealth
#goodhealthmatters
#goodhealthtoall
#goodhealthy
#goodhealthyfood
#happyhealthierme
#happyhealthyfamily
#happyhealthyfit
#happyhealthyhabits
#happyhealthylife
#happyhealthyliving
#happyhealthyme
#happyhealthyyou
#healthadvisor
#healthandbeauty
#healthandfitness
#healthandnutritious
#healthandwellnessbusiness
#healthcoach
#healthfitnessnutrition
#healthierandhappier
#healthierathome

#healthierchoices
#healthierhappierme
#healthierlifestyle
#healthierme
#healthieroptions
#healthiertogether
#healthispriority
#healthisreallywealth
#healthiswealth
#healthjourney
#healthkick
#healthquoteoftheday
#healthsecrets
#healthwise
#healthyaf
#healthybalance
#healthybody
#healthyboost
#healthyboundries
#healthybreakfast
#healthychildhealthyworld
#healthychoice
#healthycomesfirst
#healthycommunity
#healthycooking
#healthycookingandfitness
#healthydiet
#healthydietplan

#healthydinner
#healthydrink
#healthyfitandhappy
#healthyfood
#healthyfoodnut
#healthyhabits
#healthyhair
#healthyhairjourney
#healthyhydration
#healthyishappy
#healthylife
#healthyliving
#healthylovehabits
#healthylunch
#healthylunchhabits
#healthymeal
#healthymom
#healthymum
#healthynotskinny
#healthypackedlunch
#healthyrecipe
#healthyrecipeshare
#healthyrolemodels
#healthysmoothies
#healthysnack
#healthytastylifestyle
#healthywhenpossible
#healthyworkplace

COFFEE

#(city) + coffee
#(city) + coffeeshops
#blackcoffee
#booksandcoffee
#butfirstcoffee
#caffeinatedlife
#caffeineaddict
#caffeineandconquer
#caffinateandconquer
#cappuccinoart
#cappuccinotime
#coffee_time
#coffeeaddict
#coffeeaddiction
#coffeeaddicts
#coffeeaesthetic
#coffeeandchat
#coffeeandcurrentlyreading
#coffeeart
#coffeeathome
#coffeebeans
#coffeecoffeecoffee
#coffeeculture
#coffeedaily
#coffeedate

#coffeeholic
#coffeehouse
#coffeeislife
#coffeeislove
#coffelifeme
#coffeelove
#coffeemoment
#coffeemugsofinstagram
#coffeeneeded
#coffeeoclock
#coffeeoftheday
#coffeephotography
#coffeepickmeup
#coffeeplease
#coffeeroastery
#coffeeroasting
#coffeesesh
#coffeeshopcorners
#coffeeshops
#coffeeshopvibes
#coffeeshots
#coffeestyle
#coffeetimeallthetime
#coffeetimeanytime
#coffeetimeisanytime

#coffeetimeisthebesttime
#coffeetimestory
#coffeetimewithfriends
#coffeetimes
#coffeeuniverse
#coffeewithaview
#coffeewithcharacter
#coffiecup
#coldbrew
#craftcoffee
#espressolove
#espressotime
#independentcoffee
#independentcoffeeshop
#latte_art
#latteartoftheday
#latteartlicious
#latteartaddict
#lattecoffee
#lattee
#lattegram
#lattelove
#smallbatchroasting
#specialitycoffee
#whatsinmycup

TEA

#365daysoftea	#happylifewithtea	#teaconnoisseur
#acupoftea	#happysipping	#teacozy
#afternoontea	#haveacupoftea	#teaculture
#alwaystimefortea	#healthytea	#teacups
#artisantea	#herbalioustea	#teadrinkers
#blacktea	#herbalteablends	#teadrinkersofinstagram
#breakfasttea	#herbalteas	#teaenthusiast
#butfirsttea	#hottea	#teagram
#caffeinefree	#ilovetea	#teaislife
#chaiislove	#indiantea	#teaislove
#chaitime	#instatea	#tealifestyle
#chaiwithfriends	#looseleafchai	#tealovers
#cupoftea	#looseleaftea	#tealoversclub
#cupofteatime	#morningtea	#tealoversunite
#cuppatea	#morningcuppa	#teamoment
#detoxtea	#onequietcup	#teaofinstagram
#drinktea	#perfectcupoftea	#teaoftheday
#englishtea	#realchai	#teapeople
#gingertea	#refreshingtea	#teaphotography
#glassteacup	#teaaddict	#teashop
#glassteapot	#teaandbiscuits	#teastagram
#greentea	#teaandcake	#teastories
#greenteabenefits	#teaandflowers	#teatime
#greenteacake	#teaandseasons	#teatimemetime
#greentealatte	#teablogger	#teatogo
#greenteamatcha	#teaceremony	#thepoweroftea
#greenteatime	#teacommunity	#wellnesstea

HOME OFFICE

#deskaccessories
#deskdesign
#deskinspo
#deskinspiration
#deskgoals
#desklifebliss
#deskorganiser
#desksetup
#deskstyling
#desktopsetup
#gallerywallgoals
#homegoals
#homeideas
#homeinspo
#homeoffice
#homeofficedesk
#homeofficeday
#homeofficedecor
#homeofficedesign
#homeofficegoals
#homeofficeideas
#homeofficeinspiration
#homeofficeinspo
#homeofficelife
#homeofficemakeover
#homeofficeorganisation
#homeofficeoutfit
#homeofficesetup

#homeofficespace
#homeofficevibes
#homeofficeview
#homespacegoals
#howihome
#inspiremehomedecor
#mycreativeinterior
#myhometoinspire
#myhouseandhome
#mystylishspace
#nestandflourish
#officedecor
#officelife
#officespace
#onmydesk
#planneraccessories
#planneraddict
#planneraddiction
#planneraddicts
#plannergeek
#plannerjunkie
#plannerlife
#plannerlover
#plannernerd
#rusticcharm
#standingdesk
#stellarspaces
#wfhlife

#whitehome
#workfromhomeanywhere
#workfromhomebusiness
#workfromhomeday
#workfromhomelife
#workfromhomeperks
#workfromhomestyle
#workfromhometips
#workingfromhome
#workspaceinspo
#workspacery
#workspacewednesday
#officedecoration
#officeinspiration
#officegoals
#officeoffice
#officechic
#officeplants
#officesetup
#homeofficedog
#homeofficeview
#homeofficetips
#homeofficeproblems
#homeofficecat
#homeofficedays
#wfhsetup
#wfhtips
#wfhproblems

DOGS

#adorabledog
#adorabledogs
#beachpup
#bestwoofoftheday
#dailybark
#dailydogs
#dailydogsofinstagram
#dailydoseofdogs
#dailywoof
#dogbloggersociety
#dogfaces
#doggiesofinstagram
#dogmodelsearch
#dogmoments
#dogoftheweek

#dogoftheworld
#dogpicoftheday
#dogsinwilderness
#dogsinwildfeature
#dogsofficialdogs
#dogsofinstaworld
#dogsonthetrails
#dogsoutside
#dogstagraming
#dogsthatexplore
#dogsworld
#dogsworldwide
#exploremorewithdogs
#gooddogs
#happydoggo

#happydoggy
#happydoglife
#lifeofadog
#littledogsofinstagram
#mydogismybestfriend
#outdoordoglife
#pupperino
#puppytime
#sleepydogsofinstagram
#sunshinedog
#sweetdogs
#thegreatoutdogs
#thelifeofadog
#welovewalkingdog
#worldofdogs

CATS

#catasticworld
#catcatcat
#catexplorer
#cats_of_instaworld
#cats_of_the_world
#cats_today
#catsanddogs
#catsareawesome
#catsarelife
#catsarethebest
#catsareweird
#catsclub
#catscollective

#catsdaily
#catsforever
#catsforlife
#catsinboxes
#catsinstagram
#catsleep
#catsleeping
#catslifestyle
#catslove
#catsloversworld
#catsofgram
#catsoftheweek
#catstagramcat

#catstgram
#catstoday
#catstory
#catsworld
#caturdaycuties
#caturdaymorning
#caturdayvibes
#cutecatsofinstagram
#ilovemycatsomuch
#instafluffy
#lovemelovemycat
#meowdeling
#meowstagram

FOOD

#ahappyfooddance
#appetizerideas
#appetizersfordinner
#bakeitoff
#beautifulcuisine
#beautifulfood
#bestfoodfeed
#bonappetite
#breakfasttable
#brunchgoals
#cheesefordays
#cookfromscratch
#cooksillustrated
#cookstagram
#damnthatsdelish
#delicious_food
#deliciousandhealthy
#deliciousandnutritious
#deliciousbites
#deliciousdelicious
#deliciousdinner
#deliciousdishes
#deliciousfoods
#deliciouslyhealthy
#deliciousrecipes
#eatcaptureshare
#eatdelicious
#eatgoodfeelgood
#eatinghealthy
#eatingwell
#eatprettythings

#eatrealfood
#eatwhatyoulove
#firstweeat
#foodaddict
#foodadventures
#foodallergies
#foodanddrink
#foodandwine
#foodasmedicine
#foodcapturecollective
#foodcoma
#foodcritic
#fooddaily
#fooddelivery
#foodexplorer
#foodforfoodies
#foodforfuel
#foodforlife
#foodforthesoul
#foodforthought
#foodgram
#foodheaven
#foodie_features
#foodiechats
#foodiefeature
#foodieflatlays
#foodieforlife
#foodiegram
#foodielife
#foodinspiration
#foodintheair

#foodisfuel
#foodnetwork
#foodofinstagram
#foodoftheday
#foodpassion
#foodphotographyandstyling
#foodphotooftheday
#foodpleasure
#foods4thought
#foodsensitivities
#foodservice
#foodsharing
#foodshoot
#foodshopping
#foodshow
#foodsketch
#foodsofinstagram
#foodspiration
#foodspotting
#foodstagramming
#foodstalls
#foodstarz
#foodstories
#foodstreet
#foodstyleguide
#foodstyling
#foodstylingphotography
#foodstylish
#foodtography
#foodtruckfood
#forkfeed

#gloriousfood
#glutenfreedom
#glutenfreeeats
#glutenfreefoodie
#glutenfreeliving
#glutenfreelunch
#glutenfreerecipes
#glutenfreetreats
#grazingplatter
#grazingtables
#hautecusines
#hereismyfood
#homecooksofinstagram
#inmykitchen
#instafoodlover

#instafoodphoto
#instayum
#lifeandthyme
#lovewhatyoueat
#makeitdelicious
#mycommontable
#onepotmeal
#onmyplate
#ourfoodstories
#outdoordining
#quickdinners
#scrumptiouskitchen
#seriouseats
#shareyourtable
#sustainablefood

#tastespotting
#tastingtables
#thecookfeed
#theeverygirlcooks
#thefeedfeedbaking
#thefeedfeedchocolate
#thefeedfeedvegan
#thefeedfeedvegetarian
#todayfoodclub
#weddingcatering
#whatsfordinnertonight
#yougottaeatthis
#yummm
#yummyinmytummy
#yumyumyum

VEGAN

#deliciouslyvegan
#deliciousvegan
#deliciousveganfood
#happyhealthyvegan
#plantbasedbreakfast
#plantbaseddiet
#plantbasedrecipes
#tastyvegan
#tastyveganfood
#theveganclub
#tofurecipes
#veganasianfood
#veganbaking
#veganbombs
#veganbowl

#vegancake
#vegancheese
#vegancooking
#vegandeli
#vegandessert
#vegandiet
#veganfoodblog
#veganfooddiary
#veganfoods
#veganhealth
#veganideas
#veganindianfood
#veganinspiration
#veganiseasy
#veganjunkfood

#veganmeals
#veganmilkshake
#vegannutrition
#veganpancakes
#veganrecipe
#vegansmoothie
#vegansoup
#veganstreetfood
#vegansweet
#vegansweettreats
#vegantreats
#veganvibes
#veganworld
#veganworldshare
#yummyvegan

WORLD FOOD

#asiancuisine
#asianfoodfestival
#asianfoodisthebest
#asianfoodlove
#asianfoodrecipes
#asianfoodshare
#asianfoodstyle
#authenticchinesecuisine
#authenticchinesefood
#authenticindiancuisine
#authenticindiancurry
#authenticindianfood
#authenticmexicanfood
#authenticthaifood
#basmatirice
#brownstewchicken
#caribbeancuisine
#caribbeanfoodie
#chickencurry
#chickenfriedrice
#chillipaneer
#chinesecuisine
#chinesefoodlover
#cuisineworld
#curryandrice
#currybeef
#currychicken
#curryclub
#curryfamily
#curryinahurry
#curryleaves

#currylovers
#currynight
#currypaste
#curryrecipe
#curryrice
#currysauce
#curryscrimp
#currystagram
#currytraveler
#eatingthecaribbean
#flavoursofindia
#goodfoodindia
#greenthaicurry
#indianbreakfast
#indiancuisine
#indiandelicacy
#indiandish
#indianfoodiesquad
#indianlunch
#indianrecipes
#italiancuisine
#jamaicancuisine
#jamaicanfood
#japanesecuisine
#koreancooking
#koreancuisine
#malaysiancuisine
#muttoncurry
#pakistanicooking
#palakpaneer
#paneerbuttermasala

#paneerlove
#paneerrecipes
#paneertikka
#punjabicooking
#redthaicurry
#riceandpeas
#ricenoodles
#ricerolls
#southindianfood
#spicychicken
#spicyfoodlover
#stewchicken
#streetchaat
#streetfoodaroma
#streetfoodaroundtheworld
#streetfoodathome
#streetfoodfestival
#streetfoodi
#streetfoodies
#streetfoodindia
#streetfoodindonesia
#streetfoodlove
#streetfoodofindia
#streetfoods
#streetfoodstories
#streetfoodstyle
#tarkadaal
#thaicurry
#vietnamesecuisine
#westindianfood
#worldfoods

WEDDING

#adventerouswedding

#allloveisequal

#beautifulbride

#belovedweddingstories

#bohoinspiration

#bohowedding

#bridalinspo

#bridalshoot

#brideandgroom

#bridetrends

#chicwedding

#creativewedding

#dancingwithher

#destinationwedding

#elopementwedding

#engagedandinspired

#fineartphotography

#fineartwedding

#fineartweddings

#firstandlasts

#forthewildlyinlove

#futuremrs

#gettinghitched

#gettingready

#happyhearts

#helloelopement

#heywildweddings

#hippiebride

#hippiewedding

#husbandandhusband

#indiebride

#indiewedding

#intimatewedding

#junebugwedding

#lgbtwedding

#loveauthentic

#loveintentionally

#loveislove

#luxewedding

#luxurywedding

#makemoments

#modernwedding

#momentsovermountains

#offbeatbride

#ohsoperfectproposal

#ontrendweddings

#plussizebride

#realwedding

#rocknrollbride

#rusticwedding

#samesexweddings

#stylemepretty

#stylishweddings

#tablestyling

#thebelovedstories

#thedailywedding

#theweddinglegends

#togetherjournal

#togetherweroam

#twobrides

#twogrooms

#urbanweddingideas

#vintagewedding

#wanderingweddings

#weddingchicks

#weddingdayready

#weddingdecor

#weddingdetails

#weddingexitinspiration

#weddingfashion

#weddingflowers

#weddinghair

#weddingideas

#weddinginspiration

#weddinginspo

#weddingpictures

#weddingreception

#weddingseason

#weddingshoes

#weddingstoryteller

#wedmegood

#wifeandwife

#wifeyforlifey

#wildloveadventures

IT'S ALL ABOUT HASHTAGS

Days & Seasons

MONDAY

#magicmonday
#manicmonday
#manicuremonday
#mantramonday
#marketingmonday
#maxoutmonday
#meatlessmonday
#mellowmonday
#memorymonday
#meowmonday
#mindfulmonday
#mindfulnessmonday
#mondayafternoon

#mondayagain
#mondayblues
#mondayevening
#mondayfeels
#mondayfunday
#mondaygoals
#mondaymadness
#mondaymantra
#mondaymemories
#mondaymiles
#mondaymindset
#mondaymonday
#mondaymood

#mondaymorning
#mondaymotivation
#mondaymotivations
#mondaymuse
#mondaymusings
#mondayoutfit
#mondaypost
#mondayrun
#mondaythoughts
#moodboardmonday
#moralmonday
#motivationmonday
#musicmonday

TUESDAY

#charitytuesday
#feelgoodtuesday
#goodnewstues
#goodnewstuesday
#howtotuesday
#itssimplytuesday
#lovetuesdays
#takemebacktuesday
#tastingtuesday
#tastytuesday
#techtuesday
#temptingtuesday
#testimionaltuesday
#texturetuesday
#timehoptuesday

#tiptuesday
#toasttuesday
#toneituptuesday
#tongueouttuesday
#transformationtuesday
#traveltuesday
#trendytuesday
#truthfultuesday
#tuesdayafternoon
#tuesdayblues
#tuesdayevening
#tuesdayfun
#tuesdaymorning
#tuesdayquotes
#tuesdayselfie

#tuesdayshoesday
#tuesdaystogether
#tuesdaytasting
#tuesdaythoughts
#tuesdaytip
#tuesdaytransformation
#tuesdaytreat
#tuesdaytrivia
#tuesdaytruth
#tuesdaytunes
#tuesdaytunesday
#tuesdayworkout
#tunetuesday
#twittertuesday
#twoforonetuesday

WEDNESDAY

#brightwhitewednesday
#happywednesday
#humpday
#humpdaywednesday
#lastwednesday
#middleoftheweek
#wackywednesday
#wallpaperwednesday
#waybackwednesday
#weddingwednesday
#wednesdayafternoon
#wednesdayfeels

#wednesdayfun
#wednesdaygrind
#wednesdayhumpday
#wednesdayinspiration
#wednesdaylove
#wednesdaymorning
#wednesdaymotivation
#wednesdayspecial
#wednesdayswewearpink
#wednesdayvibe
#wednesdaywewearpink
#wednesdaywisdom

#wednesdaywords
#wellnesswednesday
#wendesdayevening
#whateverwednesday
#wildlifewednesday
#winesday
#winewednesday
#wisdomwednesday
#wisewordswednesday
#wishfulwednesday
#woofwednesday
#wordlesswednesday

THURSDAY

#artthursday
#connectthursday
#historythursday
#ilovethursdays
#thankfulthursday
#thinkaboutitthursday
#thinkpositivethursday
#thirstythursday
#thoughtfulthursday
#throwbackthursday
#thursdate
#thursdayafternoon
#thursdaydinner

#thursdayevening
#thursdayfeeling
#thursdayfunday
#thursdaygrind
#thursdaygrind
#thursdayinspiration
#thursdaylove
#thursdaymood
#thursdaymorning
#thursdaynightfun
#thursdaynightlive
#thursdaypost
#thursdayquotes

#thursdayspecial
#thursdaystyle
#thursdaythought
#thursdaythoughts
#thursdaythrowback
#thursdaytips
#thursdaytreat
#thursdaytruth
#thursdayvibes
#thursdaywisdom
#thursdayworkout
#transformationthursday
#whatdoyouthinkthursday

FRIDAY

#adminfriday
#factfriday
#failfriday
#fanartfriday
#fashionfriday
#fearlessfriday
#featurefriday
#feelgoodfriday
#fictionfriday
#fitfriday
#fitnessfriday
#flashbackfriday
#floralfriday
#foodiefriday

#freebiefriday
#fridayafternoon
#fridayeve
#fridayevening
#fridayfact
#fridayfavourites
#fridayfeeling
#fridayfeelz
#fridayflashback
#fridayflowers
#fridayfowl
#fridayfreeforall
#fridayfun
#fridayfunday

#fridayiminlove
#fridayintroductions
#fridaymorning
#fridaynightout
#fridaynightvibes
#fridayreads
#fridaytreat
#fridayvibes
#friendfriday
#funfactfriday
#goodnewsfriday
#motivationfriday
#tgifriday
#tgifridaysuk

WEEKEND

#itstheweekendbaby
#theweekendishere
#weekendactivity
#weekendantics
#weekendathome
#weekendbreak
#weekendbrunch
#weekendchills
#weekendcountdown
#weekenddetox
#weekenddiscover
#weekendeats
#weekendescape
#weekendfun

#weekendgetaway
#weekendgetaways
#weekendin
#weekendin + (your city)
#weekending
#weekendinspiration
#weekendishere
#weekendisnear
#weekendlife
#weekendlove
#weekendmode
#weekendmodeon
#weekendnonstop
#weekendoff

#weekendoffer
#weekendproject
#weekendretreat
#weekendstories
#weekendstroll
#weekendtime
#weekendtreats
#weekendvibes
#weekendwalks
#weekendwanders
#weekendwarrior
#weekendwellspent
#weekendwisdom
#weekendworkout

SATURDAY

#happysaturdayfolks
#happysaturdaynight
#happysaturdays
#happysaturdayeveryone
#salessaturday
#saturdaybaking
#saturdaybreakfast
#saturdaybrunch
#saturdaycoffee
#saturdaycooking
#saturdayfeeling
#saturdayfeels
#saturdayinspiration
#saturdaylife

#saturdaylook
#saturdaylove
#saturdaymarket
#saturdaymorning
#saturdaymorningvibes
#saturdaynightfever
#saturdaynightout
#saturdaynightselfie
#saturdaynightvibes
#saturdayparty
#saturdayrun
#saturdaysareforweddings
#saturdayselfies
#saturdayshenanigans

#saturdayshopping
#saturdayshoutout
#saturdaysnuggles
#saturdayspecial
#saturdaystyle
#saturdaysuperstars
#saturdayswag
#saturdaysweat
#saturdaythoughts
#saturdaywalk
#saturdayz
#saturyay
#selfiesaturday
#spotlightsaturday

SUNDAY

#lazysunday
#lazysundaymorning
#sciencesunday
#selfcaresunday
#selfiesunday
#selflesssunday
#shelfiesunday
#sundaybaking
#sundaybest
#sundayblog
#sundaybrunch
#sundaychill
#sundaycooking
#sundaydinner

#sundayfeels
#sundayfootball
#sundayfunday
#sundayhike
#sundayinspiration
#sundayleague
#sundaymarket
#sundaymealprep
#sundaymornings
#sundaymotivation
#sundaynights
#sundaypost
#sundayquote
#sundayread

#sundayreading
#sundayrun
#sundaysessions
#sundayshopping
#sundaysnuggles
#sundayspecial
#sundaysupper
#sundaysweat
#sundaythoughts
#sundaytimes
#sundayvibe
#sundaywalks
#sundayworkout
#sundayz

SEASONS

#amonthoflovely

#aseasonalshift

#autumndays

#autumninmyheart

#autumniscoming

#autumnlove

#autumnmood

#autumnstyle

#autumnwedding

#capturingseasons

#christmascheer

#christmasisnear

#christmaslove

#christmastradition

#coffeeandseasons

#colorsofspring

#createinspring

#decorbetweentheseasons

#doortomywonderland

#easteriscoming

#eastertime

#embracingtheseasons

#facethespring

#favtimeoftheday

#feelslikesummer

#getreadyforautumn

#getreadyforspring

#getreadyforsummer

#getreadyforwinter

#ilovethesunshine

#inbetweenseasons

#lovingthesun

#lovingtheweather

#makingthemostofthesun

#melodiesofspring

#myseasonalstory

#mywintercapture

#needsomefreshair

#savouringtheseasons

#seasonalpoetry

#seasonsandlandscapes

#seasonschange

#seasonschanging

#seasonsfest

#seasonsfordecor

#seasonsgreetings

#seasonsinthesun

#seasonsoflife

#seasonsoflove

#seasonsofsimplicity

#seasonspoetry

#slowsimpleseason

#slowsummerdays

#soakingupthesun

#soreadyforspring

#springcleaning

#springcollection

#springfeelings

#springready

#springwatch

#stylingtheseasons

#summerbreak

#summerfeels

#summerglow

#summergoals

#summerlife

#summerlove

#summerrain

#summerreading

#summerready

#summersunselection

#summertimes

#summertimesadness

#summertrends

#summervibe

#sunnydaysarethebest

#sunshinefuntime

#sunshinetherapy

#sunshinetime

#sunshinyday

#teaandseasons

#thatwinterspringthing

#thebeautyinspring

#winterclassic

#winterlookslikethis

#wintervibes

#winterwonderland

IT'S ALL ABOUT HASHTAGS

Business

BUSINESS GENERAL

#9tothrive
#bestinbusiness
#beyourownboss
#buildyourempire
#businessandpleasure
#businessbooks
#businessbuilder
#businesscarddesign
#businesscoaching
#businessconsultant
#businessestogether
#businessgrowthtips
#businessideas
#businessintelligence
#businesslaunch
#businesslife
#businessmanagement

#businessmarketing
#businessmind
#businessmindset
#businessnetworking
#businessonline
#businessownerlife
#businesspassion
#businessplanning
#businessquote
#businessstrategist
#businesstalk
#businesswithheart
#butthatsnoneofmybusiness
#conciousbusiness
#diversityinbusiness
#facebehindthebusiness
#familybusiness

#freedombusiness
#freelancetofreedom
#growbizfast
#growyourbusiness
#handmadebusiness
#heartcentredbusiness
#homebasedbusiness
#intentionalbusiness
#introvertedboss
#investinyourbusiness
#knowliketrust
#lovemybiz
#mindfulbusiness
#mindingmybusiness
#onlinebusiness
#progressoverperfection
#workonthego

BUSINESS GOALS

#beingboss
#betheceo
#beyourownboss
#businessgoals
#businessgrind
#businesssuccess
#ceomindset
#dreambigorgohome
#freedombasedbusiness
#freelancelife

#goaldigging
#goalgettermindset
#goalplanning
#handsandhustle
#heartcentredbusiness
#keytosuccess
#knowliketrust
#laptoplifestyle
#livelifeonyourterms
#lovemybiz

#plannersgonnaplan
#riseandgrind
#risingtidesociety
#savvybusinessowner
#startupgrind
#successfulbusiness
#targetaudience
#workanywhere
#workforwhatyouwant
#workforyourdream

ENTREPRENEUR

#aspiringentrepreneur
#bosslifestyle
#bossmindset
#bossmode
#bossmoves
#bosstalk
#ceolife
#ceolifestyle
#ceointhemaking
#ceoofme
#ceoofmylife
#ceomindset
#consciousleadership
#entrepreneuress
#entrepreneurfamily
#entrepreneurforlife

#entrepreneurgoals
#entrepreneurhubclub
#entrepreneurialmindset
#entrepreneurinthemaking
#entrepreneurjourney
#entrepreneurlife
#entrepreneurlifestyle
#entrepreneurlove
#entrepreneurmind
#entrepreneurmindset
#entrepreneurmotivation
#entrepreneurship101
#entrepreneurshipfacts
#entrepreneurshipschool
#entrepreneursinreallife
#entrepreneursofinstagram

#entrepreneurspirit
#entrepreneursruletheworld
#entrepreneurstyle
#entrepreneursunite
#entrepreneurteam
#entrepreneurtips
#entrepreneuruk
#highvibeentrepeneur
#instabossmob
#introvertentrepreneur
#justboss
#slowentrepreneur
#solopreneur
#solopreneurlife

HAPPY CLIENTS

#amazingclients
#awesomeclients
#bestclients
#bestclientsever
#clientfeedback
#clientreview
#clientslist
#clientsmatter
#clienttestimonial

#greatclients
#happyclientdiaries
#happyclienthappylife
#happyclienthappyme
#happyclientshappyme
#happyclienthappystylist
#happycustomer
#happywords
#ihavethebestclients

#ilovewhatido
#kindwords
#lovemycareer
#lovemyclients
#myclientsrock
#satisfiedclient
#testimonials
#testimonialthursday
#testimonialtuesday

FEMALE ENTREPRENEUR

#beingboss
#beyourownboss
#bossbabe
#bossbabetribe
#bosschick
#bossgirlcertified
#bossladymindset
#bossladystatus
#bossladiesmindset
#buildingbossladies
#businessbabe
#businesschicks
#businessgirl
#businessinheels
#businesswomen
#ceomum
#creativeentrepreneurs
#creativewoman
#empowerher
#entrepreneurher
#entrepreneurlifestyle
#entrepreneurwoman
#femaleentrepreneurlife

#femaleentrepreneurs
#femalefounders
#femalestartup
#fempire
#fempreneur
#femtrepreneur
#fewpower
#fiercefemales
#freedombusiness
#freelancingfemales
#girlboss
#girlbosses
#girlbossesunite
#girlbossgang
#girlbossparty
#girlpreneur
#herbusiness
#hersuccess
#iamtheeverygirl
#igbusinesswoman
#ladiesinbiz
#ladiesinbusiness
#ladieswholaunch

#ladyboss
#ladybosslifestyle
#ladystartups
#leadinglady
#motivatingwomen
#powerwomen
#sheboss
#sheconquers
#sheeo
#shemeansbusiness
#startupwomen
#staybossyladies
#thisgirlmeansbusiness
#wearerare
#womanceo
#womanceomindset
#womanofimpact
#womanonamission
#womanwithaplan
#womenbusinessowners
#womenceo
#womenceomindset
#womenconnect

MUMS IN BUSINESS

#bossmomlife
#bossmoms
#bossmomsinspire
#businessmoms
#businessmum
#businessmumma
#businessmumnetwork
#busymama
#creativemotherhood
#lifeofaworkingmum
#mamaboss
#mamabusiness
#mammanetworker
#modernmama
#mombiz
#momboss

#momhustle
#mompreneurlife
#mompreneurs
#mompreneurship
#momswhowork
#motherhoodlife
#motherhoodunplugged
#motherhustler
#multitaskingmum
#mumbosses
#mumbosslife
#mumbusiness
#muminbusiness
#mumlifeuk
#mumming
#mumpreneur

#mumsinbusiness
#mumsnet
#mumssupportingmums
#mumswhoworkfromhome
#raisingtinyhumans
#stylishmum
#thejuggleisreal
#wfhmum
#workingmomguilt
#workingmomlife
#workingmommylife
#workingmomproblems
#workingmomprobs
#workingmomtips
#workingmum
#workingmumlife

LEADERSHIP & TRAINING

#businesscoaching
#businessdevelopment
#businessmentoring
#consciousleadership
#executiveleadership
#followtheleader
#leadershipandhearts
#leadershipchallenge
#leadershipdevelopment
#leadershiplessons
#leadershipmentoring
#leadershipteam

#leadershipteamdevelopment
#managementtraining
#mentorship
#selfmanagement
#softskillstraining
#teamdevelopment
#trainingacademy
#traininganddevelopment
#trainingbuddies
#trainingbuddy
#trainingcamp
#trainingcourse

#trainingdays
#trainingeveryday
#trainingforlife
#traininggoals
#traininginspiration
#traininglife
#trainingmode
#trainingmotivation
#trainingpartner
#trainingschool
#trainingsession
#trainingwarriors

LEARNING & WORKSHOPS

#deeplearning
#educationfordesigners
#floralworkshop
#foodstylingworkshop
#freemasterclass
#freeworkshop
#handsonlearning
#knittingworkshop
#learninganddevelopment
#learnandearn
#learningart
#learningathome
#learningbydoing
#learningcurve
#learningeveryday
#learningexperience
#learningforlife
#learningfromhome

#learningisfun
#learningjourney
#learningmadefun
#learningneverstops
#learningnewskills
#learningnewthings
#learningonline
#learningphotography
#learningprocess
#learningresources
#learningtime
#learningtogether
#learningtolovemyself
#learnoutdoors
#learnthroughplay
#lovetolearn
#masterclass
#masterclassday

#masterclasses
#moodboardworkshop
#onlinelearning
#onlineworkshop
#schoolofthought
#sewingworkshop
#socialmediaworkshop
#visionboardworkshop
#webinar
#webinarmarketing
#webinaronline
#webinars
#webinarseries
#webinarwednesday
#wellbeingworkshops
#workshopbrand
#workshopday
#workshopforcreatives

CAREER & RECRUITMENT

#careerbuilder
#careerchanges
#careercoach
#careercoaching
#careercounselling
#careerlife
#careerpath
#careerplanning
#careertipsdaily
#coverletters
#employmentopportunity
#interviewcoach
#interviewing

#interviewoutfit
#interviewprep
#interviewpreparation
#interviewready
#interviewskills
#interviewtechniques
#interviewtips
#jobadvice
#jobinterviewhelp
#jobinterviewtoday
#jobsearchadvice
#jobsearchtips
#newcareergoal

#newcareermove
#newcareeropportunities
#newcareerpath
#newjobopportunity
#newjobplease
#newjobsearch
#newjobstartsmonday
#personaldevelopment
#recruitmentagency
#recruitmentlife
#resumemakeover
#resumeservices
#transferableskills

NETWORKS & COLLABORATIONS

#buildyourtribe

#businesscommunity

#businessconnections

#collaborate

#collaborationbeer

#collaborationbringsperfection

#collaborationforlife

#collaborationiskey

#collaborationnotcompetition

#collaborationovercompetition

#collaborationproject

#collaborationrocks

#collaborationstation

#collaborationwithnature

#collaborationwork

#communitybuilding

#communityovercompetiton

#communitylove

#connections

#connecting

#corevalues

#empowereachother

#findyourflock

#helpothers

#inspireconnectgrow

#letsworktogether

#likeattractslike

#makeanimpact

#networking + (your city)

#networking101

#networkingatitsbest

#networkingbrunch

#networkingbusiness

#networkingconference

#networkingday

#networkingdoneright

#networkingevent

#networkingfun

#networkinggroup

#networkingideas

#networkinginstyle

#networkingisthekey

#networkingking

#networkingnetwork

#networkingneverends

#networkingqueen

#networkingsolutions

#networkingsuperstars

#networkingtimes

#networkingtips

#networkingtraffic

#sisterhoodovercompetition

#supportoneanother

#togetherwearestronger

#workingtogether

#worktogether

MARKETING & PR

#adagency
#businessconsulting
#businessgrowthtips
#businesslaunch
#businessnews
#contentmarketingtips
#digitalmarketing101
#digitalmarketingblog
#digitalmarketingconsultant
#digitalmarketingexpert
#digitalmarketinglife
#digitalmarketingstrategy
#digitalmarketingtip
#digitalmarketingtools
#digitalmarketingtraining
#digitalmarketingtrends
#digitalpr
#emailmarketing
#emailmarketingcampaigns
#emailmarketingmanager
#emailmarketingstats
#emailmarketingstrategy
#emailmarketingtips
#listbuilding

#listbuildingsecrets
#listbuildingstrategy
#listbuildingtips
#marketigdesign
#marketing101
#marketing360
#marketingadvice
#marketingagency
#marketingcampaign
#marketingcoach
#marketingconsultant
#marketingdigital
#marketingexpert
#marketinggenius
#marketinggoals
#marketingguru
#marketinginstagram
#marketingislife
#marketinglife
#marketingmentor
#marketingsavvy
#marketingservcies
#marketingsocial
#marketingspecialist

#marketingstrategy
#marketingteam
#marketingtip
#mediaagency
#mediamarketing
#mediarelations
#onlinemarketing
#pr101
#pragency
#prguru
#prjobs
#prlife
#publicist
#publicrelationsagency
#publicrelationsconsultant
#publicrelationsfirm
#publicrelationslife
#publicrelationsprofessional
#publicrelationsspecialist
#publicrelationsstrategy
#publicrelationstips
#socialcurator
#strategicmarketing
#womeninpr

FREELANCING

#artconsultant
#beautyconsultant
#brandconsultant
#brandingconsultant
#businessconsultant
#consultantlife
#consultants
#designerfreelancer
#digitalmarketingconsultant
#educationconsultant
#escape9to5
#escapethe9to5
#fashionconsultant
#foodconsultant
#freelancecopywriter
#freelancedesigner
#freelancefashiondesigner
#freelancefriday
#freelancegraphicdesign
#freelanceillustrator
#freelancejobs
#freelancelife
#freelancemarketing
#freelancemodel
#freelancephotographer
#freelancephotography
#freelanceragency

#freelancerartist
#freelanceratwork
#freelancerdesign
#freelancerdesigner
#freelancereporter
#freelancerforhire
#freelancerfreedom
#freelancergraphicdesigner
#freelancerhelp
#freelancerillustrator
#freelancerjob
#freelancerlife
#freelancerlifestyle
#freelancermakeupartist
#freelancerproblems
#freelancers
#freelancerslife
#freelancersofig
#freelancersofinstagram
#freelancersunite
#freelancertips
#freelancerwriter
#freelancestylist
#freelancetofreedom
#freelancewisdom
#freelancewriter
#freelancingfemales

#goodbye9to5
#imageconsultant
#itconsultant
#itconsulting
#marketingconsultant
#myownboss
#no9to5
#nomore9to5
#nutritionconsultant
#quit9to5
#quityour9to5
#secondincome
#selfemployedinspiration
#selfemployedlife
#selfemployment
#smallbusinessconsultant
#styleconsultant
#travelconsultant
#virtualassistant
#virtualassistantlife
#virtualassistantservices
#virtualpa
#virtualservices + (your city)
#workforyourself
#workingfromwifi
#workonthego
#workthatworks

SMALL BUSINESS

#dreamsmallbiz

#knowliketrust

#mysmallbiz

#mysmallbizwhy

#smallandmightybiz

#smallandmightybusiness

#smallbiz + (your city)

#smallbizbloom

#smallbizconnect

#smallbizfamily

#smallbizlife

#smallbizlove

#smallbizmarketing

#smallbiznetworking

#smallbizowner

#smallbizsatuk

#smallbizsaturday

#smallbizservices

#smallbizshout

#smallbizsocialmedia

#smallbizsquad

#smallbizstory

#smallbizsuccess

#smallbizsupport

#smallbizsupportingsmallbiz

#smallbiztips

#smallbizuk

#smallbizlife

#smallbizweek

#smallbusiness + your city

#smallbusinessadvice

#smallbusinessbigdreams

#smallbusinessboss

#smallbusinesscoach

#smallbusinessconsultant

#smallbusinessentrepreneur

#smallbusinessgrowth

#smallbusinesslife

#smallbusinessloan

#smallbusinesslove

#smallbusinessmarketingtips

#smallbusinessmatters

#smallbusinessopportunity

#smallbusinessowner

#smallbusinessrevolution

#smallbusinessrocks

#smallbusinesssaturday

#smallbusinessstartup

#smallbusinessstrategy

#smallbusinesssupport

#smallbusinesstips

#smallbusinessuk

#startupbusiness

#supportsmallbusinessowners

INDEPENDENT SHOP OWNER

#buyindependent

#buylessbuybetter

#campaignshopindependent

#consciousconsumer

#ihavethisthingwithshops

#independentbusiness

#indiebusiness

#indieretail

#madein + (your city)

#sharingaworldofshops

#shopescenes

#shopinde

#shopindependent

#shopindependentthischristmas

#shopindie

#shopkeepers

#shoplocally

#shoppingwithsoul

#shopscenes

#shopindependent

#shoplocal + (your city)

#shoplocaluk

#shopsmall

#shopsmallbusiness

#shopsmall_(your city)

#shopsmallbiz

#shopsmalllove

#shopsmallsaturday

#shopsmalluk

#shopviews

#storefrontcollective

#supportindependent

#supportinglocalbusiness

#supportingsmall

#supportingsmallbiz

#supportingsmallbusiness

#supportingsmallbusinesses

#supportlocalmakers

#supporttheindependents

#supportyourhighstreet

#theindependentshopkeepers

#theshopkeepers

COACHING

#abundancecoach
#accountabilitypartner
#agilecoaching
#bethechangeyouwanttosee
#bizcoach
#boldbraveyou
#buildalifeyoulove
#businessbydesign
#businesscoach
#businesscoaching
#businesscoaching101
#businesscoachingforwomen
#businesscoachingonline
#businessmentoring
#careeradvancement
#coachesofinstagram
#coaching101
#coaching24_7
#coachingclasses
#coachingforlife
#coachingforwomen
#coachinggroup
#coachinglife
#coachinglifestyle
#coachingonline
#coachingparental
#coachingpersonal
#coachingquotes
#coachingtime
#coachingtips
#coachingworks

#coachlife
#cultivatewhatmatters
#executivecoaching
#executivecoaching
#fearoffailure
#femalebusinesscoach
#findingyourfearless
#findyourflow
#findyourpurposeinlife
#fitnesscoaching
#goalcrusher
#goalgetter
#goalplanning
#goalsetter
#goatyourownpace
#gratitudeattitude
#healthcoaching
#inspiredtoimpact
#instacoaching
#instagramcoach
#intentionalbusiness
#investinginmyself
#knowyourwhy
#lawofattractioncoaching
#leadershipcoaching
#learnandearn
#lifecoach
#lifecoachforwomen
#lifecoaching
#lifecoachingformen
#littlebylittle

#liveyourpassion
#mentalcoach
#mindsetcoaching
#mindsetgrowth
#mindsetshift
#motivationaltips
#performancecoaching
#personalbrandingcoach
#personaldevelopmentcoach
#personalgrowthtips
#planyourlife
#positivecoaching
#productivitycoach
#purposedrivenlife
#salescoaching
#sayyestosuccess
#selfdevelopmenttools
#setagoal
#sharewhatyouknow
#smallbizcoach
#smartgoals
#startwithwhy
#stopprocrastinating
#storytellingcoach
#strategicplanning
#thinkgrowprosper
#trainyourmind
#uplevelyourlife
#weeklyplanning
#womanwithaplan
#worksmarternotharder

IT'S ALL ABOUT HASHTAGS

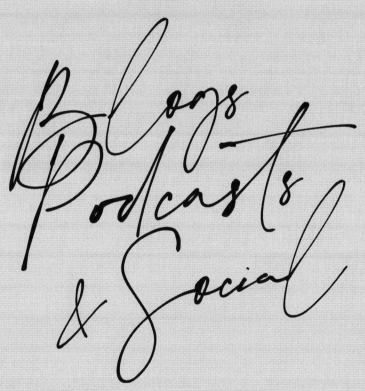

BLOGGING

#(your city) + blogger
#blackmomsblog
#blackmomswhoblog
#beautybloggerlife
#beautybloggeruk
#beautyblogging
#beautyblogs
#blogboss
#blogfood
#bloggerbabe
#bloggerdiaries
#bloggerin
#bloggerlife
#bloggerlifestyle
#bloggerlove
#bloggermama
#bloggermom
#bloggernation
#bloggerproblems
#bloggersgetsocial
#bloggerslife
#bloggersofinstagram
#bloggerstribe
#bloggerstyle
#bloggerswanted
#bloggertips
#bloggeruk
#bloggervibes
#bloggersunder5k

#bloggingbabes
#bloggingboss
#blogginggals
#blogginglife
#bloggingmum
#bloggingtips
#blogilates
#bloglife
#blogliferules
#bloglifetogether
#bloglifestyle
#bloglinkinbio
#bloglinkinprofile
#bloglovin
#blogpromotion
#blogtravel
#blogtrip
#businessblog
#businessblogger
#businessblogging
#careerblogger
#creativeblog
#creativeblogger
#designblog
#designblogger
#foodblogeats
#foodbloggerlife
#foodbloggerpro
#foodblogging

#foodblogs
#howtoblog
#instablogger
#interiorsblogger
#mombloggercommunity
#mombloggerlife
#mombloggers
#mombloginfluence
#momblogs
#momblogtribe
#mumblog
#mumblogger
#mumbloggeruk
#newblogger
#newblogpost
#newblogpostalert
#newblogposts
#newontheblog
#ontheblogtoday
#personalblogger
#problogging
#stationeryblogger
#thebloggershub
#theblogissue
#ukblogger
#veganblogger
#weddingblogger
#wellnessblogger
#writeyourblog

PODCASTS

#applepodcasts

#blackpodcastersofinstagram

#businesspodcast

#creativepodcast

#designpodcast

#entrepreneurpodcast

#googlepodcasts

#ilovepodcasting

#instaepisode

#instalistening

#instapodcast

#instapodcasts

#marketingpodcast

#millennialpodcast

#mompodcast

#photographypodcast

#podcastaddict

#podcastawards

#podcastcomingsoon

#podcastcommunity

#podcastdesign

#podcastdiva

#podcastepisode

#podcasterofinstagram

#podcastersofinstagram

#podcastfamily

#podcastfan

#podcastforfoodies

#podcastfriday

#podcastgal

#podcastguest

#podcasthost

#podcasting

#podcastingisfun

#podcastinglifestyle

#podcastingnews

#podcastingtips

#podcastinterview

#podcastjunkie

#podcastlife

#podcastlistening

#podcastlive

#podcastlove

#podcastmarketing

#podcastmonday

#podcastmovement

#podcastnetwork

#podcastnews

#podcastoftheday

#podcastphotography

#podcastproduction

#podcastqueen

#podcastrecommendation

#podcastseries

#podcastshow

#podcastsig

#podcastsponsor

#podcaststudio

#podcastuk

#podcastvibes

#podcastvideo

#podcastwebinar

#podcastwisdom

#postcast + (your city)

#postcastitunes

#spotifypodcast

SOCIAL MEDIA

#bemoresocial
#besocial
#blackcontentcreators
#collectivehub
#contentcreator
#contentcurator
#contentdevelopment
#contentmarketer
#contentmarketing
#contentmarketingtips
#contentstrategy
#digitalagencymarketing
#digitalmarketing
#digitalmarketingsolutions
#digitalmarketingstrategies
#digitalmarketingstrategy
#facebookinsights
#keepsocialmediasocial
#igstories
#igstory
#igstorytemplate
#igtips
#instagrambasics
#instagrambusiness
#instagramcoaches
#instagramcoach
#instagramforbusiness
#instagramgrowth

#instagrammanagement
#instagramstoryhacks
#instagramstoryideas
#instagramstoryinspo
#instagramtips
#instagramtipsforbusiness
#instastories
#keepsocialmediasocial
#marketingexpert
#marketingguru
#marketingideas
#onlinemarketing
#onlinemarketingtips
#onlinepresence
#pinterestforbusiness
#pinterestforthewin
#pinterestmarketing
#pinterestrockstars
#pintereststrategy
#pinterestwin
#smm
#socialcurator
#socialmedia101
#socialmediaagency
#socialmediaboss
#socialmediacoach
#socialmediaconsultant
#socialmediaconsulting

#socialmediaexperts
#socialmediaforbusiness
#socialmediagrowth
#socialmediaguru
#socialmediahelp
#socialmediainfluencer
#socialmedialife
#socialmediamanagement
#socialmediamanager
#socialmediamanagerlife
#socialmediamarketer
#socialmediamarketing
#socialmediamarketingtips
#socialmediamaven
#socialmediaoptimization
#socialmediaqueen
#socialmediastrategist
#socialmediastrategy
#socialmediasuccess
#socialmediatip
#socialmediatips
#socialmediatipsandtricks
#socialmediatools
#socialmediatrainer
#socialmediatrends
#socialselling
#socialstrategysquad
#webmarketing

IT'S ALL ABOUT HASHTAGS

Beauty Hair & Wellness

MAKEUP

#alternativemakeup
#beautyaddict
#beautygirls
#beautyhacks
#beautyobsessed
#beautyreview
#beautyroom
#beautyroutine
#beautysecret
#beautytherapy
#beautytip
#blackbeautybrands
#blackbeautymatters
#blackbeautytips
#blackbeautyqueens
#bridalmakeup
#colourcosmetics
#contouringandhighlight
#contourtutorial
#cosmeticlovers
#darkmakeup
#darkskinwomenmakeup
#dewymakeup
#eyeshadowlooks
#fullcolormakeup
#gothmakeup
#highlighting
#ilovemakeup

#instabeauty
#instamakeup
#makeupaddict
#makeupartistsworldwide
#makeupbag
#makeupblog
#makeupbyme
#makeupcollection
#makeupcollector
#makeupformelanin
#makeupfun
#makeupgirl
#makeupglam
#makeupgoals
#makeupguru
#makeuphaul
#makeuphoarder
#makeupideas
#makeupinspo
#makeupisart
#makeupislife
#makeupismylife
#makeuplife
#makeuplook
#makeuplooks
#makeuplover
#makeupmess
#makeupobsession

#makeupofig
#makeuponfleek
#makeuppage
#makeupparty
#makeupstudio
#makeuptime
#makeuptips
#makeuptutorial
#melaninbeautiesunite
#melaninmakeupdaily
#motd
#muaannouncer
#muasfam
#muaunderdogs
#muaxdiscover
#naturalmakeupartist
#naturalmakeuplook
#newmua
#nomakeuplook
#nomakeupmakeup
#nomakeupmakeuplook
#paleskinmakeup
#smokeyeye
#thecrayoncase
#undiscovered_muas
#undiscoveredmuas
#unleashyourinnerartist
#wakeupandmakeup

SEMI-PERMANENT MAKEUP

#3dbrows

#archaddicts

#browartistry

#browboss

#browlamination

#browpigmentation

#browqueen

#browsbrowsbrows

#browsspecialist

#browthreading

#cosmetictattoo

#eyebrows3d

#eyebrowshairbyhair

#eyebrowtattoo

#freshbrowfriday

#hairstrokeyebrows

#kissproof

#lipblushing

#lipbrushtattoo

#lipcolour

#lipshading

#longlastingbeauty

#longtimeliner

#masterclasspmu

#microbladedbrows

#microbladingartist

#microstroking

#nanobrows

#perfectlips

#permanenteyebrows

#permanenteyeliner

#permanentlips

#permanentmakeupartist

#phibrows

#pmuadvice

#pmuartist

#pmuexpert

#pmulips

#pmumasterclass

#pmupigment

#pmutraining

#pmuworld

#semipermanentbrows

#semipermanentlips

#semipermanentmakeup

#shadowliner

#spmubrows

#wakeupwithmakeup

NAILS

#acrylicnails
#almondnails
#amazingnails
#beautifulnailart
#beautifulnailpolish
#beautifulnails
#boldnails
#creativenails
#elegantnailart
#elegantnails
#frenchnailstyle
#freshnails
#gelnailsdesign
#glamnails
#goldnails
#gorgousnails
#ilovemynails
#ilovenails
#instagramnails
#instanails
#livelovepolish
#lovemynails
#lovenailart
#lovenaildesign
#lovenailpolish
#manicure_ideas
#manicurednails

#manicurepedicure
#manicuretime
#nailart
#naildesign
#nailextension
#nailinspiration
#nailitdaily
#naillove
#nailperfection
#nailpolishaddict
#nailpro
#nailqueenfamily
#nailqueensonly
#nails_page
#nails2inspire
#nails4today
#nailsaddict
#nailsbeauty
#nailsbyme
#nailsdesigner
#nailsdid
#nailsdonebyme
#nailsdonehairdone
#nailsdoneright
#nailselfie
#nailsinstagram
#nailsnailsnails

#nailsnude
#nailsofinsta
#nailsofinstagram
#nailsombre
#nailsoohlala
#nailspa
#nailsperfect
#nailsstyle
#nailstagram
#nailstamping
#nailstudio
#nailstylist
#nailswagg
#nailswow
#nailtechlife
#nailtechnican
#npa
#ombrenails
#ovalnails
#prettynailsrock
#professionalnailtech
#shinenails
#sparklynails
#sparklynailsmakemehappy
#summernailart
#thenailartstory
#weddingnails

EYEBROWS & LASHES

#3dbrows
#3dbrowtones
#archaddicts
#archolic
#beautygoals
#boldbrows
#browbabe
#browenvy
#browgame
#browgoals
#browguru
#browlife
#browlift
#browlove
#browqueen
#browsarelife
#browsbrowsbrows
#browshaping
#browsfordays
#browobsessed
#browsonfleek
#browsonpoint
#browspecialist
#browtattoo
#browtransformation
#eyebrowlamination
#eyebrowsculpting
#eyebrowshaping

#eyebrowtattoo
#eyelashextensions
#falselashes
#falshies
#fluffylashes
#fulllashes
#fulllashesextension
#hairbyhair
#hairstroke
#hybridbrows
#hybridlashes
#lashartist
#lashesarelife
#lashesfordays
#lashesofinstagram
#lashesonlashes
#lashesonpoint
#lashenhancement
#lashextensions
#lashgame
#lashgamestrong
#lashliftandtint
#lashlifts
#lashliftingpro
#laslifttraining
#lashobsessed
#lashstylist
#lashtech

#lovemybrows
#lovemylashes
#microblading
#microbladingartist
#microbladingboss
#microbladingworld
#ombrebrows
#perfectbrows
#perfectlashes
#perfectlasheseverytime
#perfectlasheseasymorning
#permanentcosmetics
#permanentmakeup
#phibrows
#powderbrows
#russianlashes
#russianvolume
#semipermanentlashes
#semipermanentmakeup
#spmu
#tintingeyebrows
#threading
#volumelash
#volumelashartist
#volumelashfans
#volumelashtraining
#volumelashextensions
#wakeupwithmakeup

HAIR

#(your city) + hairdresser
#amazingnaturalhair
#babylights
#balayage
#balayagehighlights
#balayageombre
#beachhair
#beachwave
#beforeafter
#bignaturalhair
#blackhairrocks
#blackhairstyles
#blessedwithcurls
#blondbraids
#blondehair
#braidstyles
#bronde
#brunette
#colourmelt
#curlsunderstood
#curlyhair
#freelancehairstylist
#fromdarktolight
#hairart
#haircolorspecialist
#haircolourexpert
#haircolourideas
#haircolourspecialist

#hairdresserhumor
#hairdresserinthemaking
#hairdresserlove
#hairdresserpower
#hairdressers
#hairdressersconnect
#hairdressersforlife
#hairdressershavemorefun
#hairdressersjournal
#hairdresserslife
#hairdressersmagic
#hairdressersofinsta
#hairdressersofinstagram
#hairdressersproblems
#hairdressersrock
#hairdressersthatslay
#hairdresserworld
#hairgoals
#hairmakeover
#hairofinstagram
#hairoftheday
#hairstyler
#hairstylesforwomen
#hairstylist
#hairstylistlife
#hairtransformation
#happyhealthyhair
#highlightedhair

#icyblonde
#instahairstyle
#instastyles
#kinksandcoils
#longcurls
#longhair
#longhairstyles
#luvyourmane
#maneinterest
#mermaidhair
#mobilehairdresser
#naturalhairdreams
#naturalhairgoals
#naturalhairloves
#naturalhairspot
#naturalhairtips
#naturallycurly
#ombrehair
#perfectcurls
#pinkhair
#prettyhair
#respectmyhair
#showmethebalayage
#straighthair
#teamnaturalhair
#trendyhair
#type4hair
#upstyle

AROMATHERAPY

#aromadiffuser
#aromatherapeutic
#aromatheraphymassage
#aromatheraphyoil
#aromatherapist
#aromatherapistintraining
#aromatherapists
#aromatherapy
#aromatherapyassociates
#aromatherapyblends
#aromatherapybracelet
#aromatherapycandles
#aromatherapydiffuser
#aromatherapyeducation
#aromatherapyforchildren

#aromatherapyjewellery
#aromatherapylovers
#aromatherapymassage
#aromatherapyoil
#aromatherapyoils
#aromatherapyproducts
#aromatherapyrecipes
#aromatherapyschool
#aromatherapyskincare
#aromatherpycandle
#aromatherpymassage
#bekindtoyourskin
#deeptissuemassage
#diffuserblends
#essentialoilblends

#essentialoilsforthewin
#essentialoilsrock
#frankincense
#herbalaromatherapist
#herbalinfusion
#holistictherapist
#hotstonesmassage
#indianheadmassage
#lavenderoil
#lemonessentialoil
#naturaloils
#oilblends
#oilylifemadesimple
#pureessentialoils
#rebalance

REFLEXOLOGY

#amazingfeet
#anxietyrelief
#babyreflexology
#backpainrelief
#childrensreflexology
#deeptissue
#easethepain
#facialreflexology
#fertilityreflexology
#footreflexology
#handreflexology
#holistichealth
#jointpain

#jointpainrelief
#kidsreflexology
#lookingafteryourself
#lovereflexology
#massagetherapylife
#mindandbody
#naturalcare
#painmanagement
#putyourfeetupandrelax
#reflexology
#reflexologyforeveryone
#reflexologylymphdrainage
#reflexologymassage

#reflexologyrocks
#reflexologytherapist
#reflexologytreatment
#reflexologyworks
#relaxationandstressfree
#relaxmassage
#roadmaptorecovery
#tailoredtherapies
#takealoadoff
#therapeuticmassage
#treatmentroom
#wellbeingjourney
#wellbeingmatters

ESTHETICIANS

#acnescarsremoval
#acnetreatment
#aestheticianlife
#antiagingfacial
#antiagingskincare
#beautifulskin
#beautybar
#beautyessentials
#beautyregime
#beautyservices
#beautyskincare
#bestskinever
#bodywax
#botanicalskincare
#byebyewrinkles
#cleanbeautyboss
#cleanbeautyrevolution
#cleanskincare
#crueltyfreebeauty
#crueltyfreeskincare
#dayspa
#deepcleansingfacial
#dermaplaning
#dryskinrrelief
#estheticianlife
#expressfacial
#facemask
#facialacne
#facialaesthetics

#facialcare
#facialdetox
#facialist
#facialkit
#facialmask
#facialmasks
#facialmassage
#facialoil
#facialpeel
#facials
#facialscrub
#facialsculpting
#facialserum
#facialskincare
#facialspa
#facialtime
#facialtreatment
#facialtreatmentessence
#facialtreatments
#facialwaxing
#finelinesandwrinkles
#freshfaced
#glowyskin
#healthyskin
#healthyskinbeautifulskin
#healthyskincare
#hydrafacialist
#hydrafacials
#hydratingskincare

#iloveskincare
#ledlighttherapy
#loveyourskin
#luxuryskincare
#luxuryspa
#massagetime
#melaninskincare
#microdermabrasionfacial
#naturalskincare
#naturalskincarelovers
#naturalskincareproduct
#naturalskincareroutine
#naturalskincarethatworks
#naturalskincaretips
#nomorewrinkles
#nonsurgicalfacelift
#nontoxicbeauty
#organicskin
#organicskincare
#over40andfabulous
#over40skincare
#pampering
#pamperyourskin
#radiantskin
#saferbeauty
#skincareaddict
#skincareadvice
#skincarebeauty
#skincarefanatic

#skincarejourney

#skincarejunkie

#skincarelover

#skincareobsessed

#skincareproducts

#skincarespecialist

#skincaresunday

#skincaretip

#skinexperts

#skinhydration

#skinrejuvenation

#skinroutine

#skintherapy

#skintreatment

#slowbeauty

#smoothskin

#spadays

#spalife

#spatime

#spatreatments

#whatsyoursecret

#wrinklesbegone

#youngerlookingskin

#youthfulglow

HASHTAG SET 1

SET NAME:

1 ....

2 ....

3 ....

4 ....

5 ....

6 ....

7 ....

8 ....

9 ....

10 ....

11 ....

12 ....

13 ....

14 ....

15 ....

16 ....

17 ....

18 ....

19 ....

20 ....

21 ....

22 ....

23 ....

24 ....

25 ....

26 ....

27 ....

28 ....

29 ....

30 ....

HASHTAG SET 2

SET NAME:

1 ....
2 ....
3 ....
4 ....
5 ....
6 ....
7 ....
8 ....
9 ....
10 ....
11 ....
12 ....
13 ....
14 ....
15 ....

16 ....
17 ....
18 ....
19 ....
20 ....
21 ....
22 ....
23 ....
24 ....
25 ....
26 ....
27 ....
28 ....
29 ....
30 ....

HASHTAG SET 3

SET NAME:

1 ....

2 ....

3 ....

4 ....

5 ....

6 ....

7 ....

8 ....

9 ....

10 ....

11 ....

12 ....

13 ....

14 ....

15 ....

16 ....

17 ....

18 ....

19 ....

20 ....

21 ....

22 ....

23 ....

24 ....

25 ....

26 ....

27 ....

28 ....

29 ....

30 ....

HASHTAG SET 4

SET NAME:

1 ....
2 ....
3 ....
4 ....
5 ....
6 ....
7 ....
8 ....
9 ....
10 ....
11 ....
12 ....
13 ....
14 ....
15 ....
16 ....
17 ....
18 ....
19 ....
20 ....
21 ....
22 ....
23 ....
24 ....
25 ....
26 ....
27 ....
28 ....
29 ....
30 ....

HASHTAG SET 5

SET NAME:

1 ....
2 ....
3 ....
4 ....
5 ....
6 ....
7 ....
8 ....
9 ....
10 ....
11 ....
12 ....
13 ....
14 ....
15 ....

16 ....
17 ....
18 ....
19 ....
20 ....
21 ....
22 ....
23 ....
24 ....
25 ....
26 ....
27 ....
28 ....
29 ....
30 ....

HASHTAG SET 6

SET NAME:

1 ....

2 ....

3 ....

4 ....

5 ....

6 ....

7 ....

8 ....

9 ....

10 ....

11 ....

12 ....

13 ....

14 ....

15 ....

16 ....

17 ....

18 ....

19 ....

20 ....

21 ....

22 ....

23 ....

24 ....

25 ....

26 ....

27 ....

28 ....

29 ....

30 ....

HASHTAG SET 7

SET NAME:

1 ....

2 ....

3 ....

4 ....

5 ....

6 ....

7 ....

8 ....

9 ....

10 ....

11 ....

12 ....

13 ....

14 ....

15 ....

16 ....

17 ....

18 ....

19 ....

20 ....

21 ....

22 ....

23 ....

24 ....

25 ....

26 ....

27 ....

28 ....

29 ....

30 ....

HASHTAG SET 8

SET NAME:

1	16 ....
2	17 ....
3	18 ....
4	19 ....
5	20 ....
6	21 ....
7	22 ....
8	23 ....
9	24 ....
10	25 ....
11	26 ....
12	27 ....
13	28 ....
14	29 ....
15	30 ....

HASHTAG SET 9

SET NAME:

1 ....

2 ....

3 ....

4 ....

5 ....

6 ....

7 ....

8 ....

9 ....

10 ....

11 ....

12 ....

13 ....

14 ....

15 ....

16 ....

17 ....

18 ....

19 ....

20 ....

21 ....

22 ....

23 ....

24 ....

25 ....

26 ....

27 ....

28 ....

29 ....

30 ....

HASHTAG SET 10

SET NAME:

1 ....
2 ....
3 ....
4 ....
5 ....
6 ....
7 ....
8 ....
9 ....
10 ....
11 ....
12 ....
13 ....
14 ....
15 ....

16 ....
17 ....
18 ....
19 ....
20 ....
21 ....
22 ....
23 ....
24 ....
25 ....
26 ....
27 ....
28 ....
29 ....
30 ....

HASHTAG
NOTES

HASHTAG
NOTES

HASHTAG
NOTES

HASHTAG
NOTES

HASHTAG
NOTES

HASHTAG
NOTES

HASHTAG
NOTES

HASHTAG
NOTES

ACKNOWLEDGEMENTS

Thank you to my family, friends and everyone who has supported me whilst I was writing this book, especially my hubby Steve who is my chief cheerleader and right hand man. He has keep me fed, made me endless cups of tea and brought me chocolate when I needed it most to keep me motivated!

To Christy and Oliver, I apologise for all the times you have had to fend for yourself and make your own dinners. For your endless patience when Mum was busy writing her book. You guys are my absolute inspiration and my reason for doing what I do.

To my mum and dad, thank you for everything, you guys are just the best, most supportive parents ever. You helped me believe since I was a little girl that I could achieve anything that I set my heart on, the sky's the limit!

To my business besties Steph Sanderson and Amber Badger, you both gave me the confidence to believe I could ever write a book in the first place. Amber, content queen, thank you so much for editing my book.

To my wonderful friend Saf Ismail who told me very firmly while I was complaining on the phone about my job, that I needed to just start! That I needed to create my own business doing what I love best, designing brands! This was on the Friday and by the following Sunday I had registered my business and launched my website.

Printed in Great Britain
by Amazon